# The GAME of WORK

# The GAME of WORK

*Chuck Coonradt with Lee Nelson*

**Liberty Press**
**Orem, Utah**

ISBN 0-936860-17-0

First printing, December 1984

# Acknowledgements

No great work is ever accomplished by the writer alone. Just as Plato had Aristotle, the concepts developed in the following pages are based on the efforts, at least in part, of those who have gone before. Napoleon Hill, in his book *Think and Grow Rich,* was the mentor for us all, and my involvement with Success Motivation Institute and its president, Paul J. Meyer, was a springboard for many of the concepts developed in this volume. Since 1971 his programs and tapes have had a profound impact upon my life and accomplishments. We have endeavored to identify specific material borrowed from all sources and wish to express an overall appreciation to the pioneers who made it possible for books like this one to be written.

# Contents

# *Foreward*

## by Lee Nelson

My first real contact with the main principle discussed in this book occurred one afternoon when the manager of the Safeway store I was working for took me into the back room and showed me three 4X8 wooden bins filled to overflowing with empty pop bottles. I was just beginning my first after–school job, earning $1.33 an hour, not a bad wage in 1958. The store was located in Walnut Creek, California.

The manager explained that the bottles needed to be sorted into cases before they could be picked up by the various vendors. He explained why there were so many bottles in the bins, that the adult clerks hated to "work bottles" and avoided the task whenever possible. That was why I was being given the job––as a 16–year–old kid I was at the bottom of the pecking order.

The manager introduced me to the corner of the back room designated for sorting bottles. He showed me where the empty cases were stored, which bottles could be combined in the same cases, and which had to be kept separate, and where the cases of empties needed to be stacked.

Just when I thought I knew all there was to know about the new task, and was ready to go to work, the manager said, "It takes most clerks one hour to do a bin. I hope you can do that well."

He looked at his watch. I looked at mine.

"Let me know when you finish the first bin." He turned and walked away.

Suddenly my work took on a new meaning. Working the bot-

9

tles was not just another job that needed to be done. A standard had been set by which my performance would be measured, with exactness. The manager was keeping score on me. I was keeping score on myself.

My palms began to sweat. I looked at the bins of bottles with new interest.

Compared to my favorite sport, basketball, the manager had put me into a real game situation and turned on the scoreboard. I flew at the bottles.

An hour and ten minutes later I finished the first bin, frustrated at my clumsiness, but confident that if I persisted I could beat the magic 60-minute barrier—the accepted standard in my new working world.

I became the regular bottle worker, and a record was kept on how long it took me to work each bin of bottles. A month later I worked three bins of bottles in one hour—three times the acceptable rate set by my fellow workers. The manager was pleased. The other workers talked about it. I believed I was possibly the fastest bottle worker in the entire Safeway chain. I was proud. Maybe the other workers knew more than me about checking, cutting meat or trimming lettuce—but I knew more about working bottles and could do my job twice as fast as anyone else in the store.

The manager of the night stocking crew heard about the kid with the fast hands and arranged for me to be assigned to him as soon as school was out. The night shift worked from 11 p.m. until 8 a.m., and my hourly wage was increased from $1.33 to $2.42 per hour.

Bill Cunningham, the manager of the night crew, was a naturally competitive individual, both on and off the job. Every task was a race to see who was the best and the fastest.

My eyes couldn't follow Bill's price marker as it flew over the cans. He could throw six soup cans at a time onto the shelf, three in each hand, the labels all facing forward when the cans came to rest. On Tuesday nights when we washed and waxed the floors, Bill's mop could perform more tricks than a witch's broom. He learned that in the Navy.

Bill challenged me to try to keep up with him, which appeared an impossible task. But I tried and every week got a little closer. It seemed every task was timed and measured, including the tearing up of boxes for the incinerator. Speed and accuracy were the game, and we kept score. Some of the other night crew members didn't like to race with Bill and me. They thought we were too "gung ho." They seemed to prefer watching the clock instead of beating it.

10

Nothing felt better than to walk out of that store into the morning sunshine, my body winding down after a night of running full speed in an effort to keep up with or beat Bill. And when Bill would say in parting, "Big load coming in today, wear your runnin' shoes tonight," it was music to my ears. I felt like an athlete getting ready for the big game.

I went on to finish college, marry, and begin a career in business and writing. In college and future jobs the things I had learned at Safeway didn't seem to apply. There was a difference between beating records and beating people. Being fast wasn't necessarily a desirable quality if you weren't doing the right thing. Sometimes I sensed a lack of direction, even confusion, among my fellow workers. And I was at a loss how to apply in different situations the principles that had worked so well at Safeway.

Then I met Chuck Coonradt, a professional businessman who had taken the principles that had motivated me so effectively at Safeway and learned to apply them to all types of business situations, achieving phenomenal results.

Chuck is the founder of Western Leadership Group, a company that teaches executives how to turn business into a game, how to keep score. Chuck has figured out how to do for all kinds of businesses what those managers at Safeway did for me. There is no doubt in my mind that Chuck is the world's leading measurement expert.

As a sports enthusiast and a former college football player, Chuck has observed that people will pay for the privilege of working harder than they will work for pay. Think about it—we call it recreation.

"In the absence of clearly defined goals, people are forced to concentrate on activity and ultimately become enslaved by it," says Chuck. He continues, "Most businesses pay for attendance when they need to be paying for performance and productivity. Most businesspeople don't keep score, don't measure performance as effectively as they do in recreation."

As Chuck began to tell me about his experiences with many companies, I realized that he was onto something big, something very American, something vital to the success of every business. Chuck has discovered the missing link of all the goal–setting rhetoric of the '60s and '70s. I was amazed at his track record. This stuff really works. Following are brief descriptions of some of the success stories discussed in this book.

*A March-of-Dimes telethon director* developed a simple tracking system, based on dollars raised instead of people contacted—a tracking system that could be updated every hour

11

throughout the telethon. With the new system in place, donations were increased from $78,000 to $110,000 in one year. Within three years the telethon went from less than $80,000 a year to well over $200,000 a year.

A *local beverage distributor* began to measure the number of cases delivered per gallons of gas consumed in delivery trucks, and experienced an immediate 22% decrease in delivery costs.

A *manufacturing firm,* within six weeks of introducing one of Chuck's measurement techniques in a key manufacturing process, reduced the amount of scrap or wasted material from two bins a day to two bins a week, resulting in an annual savings of over $30,000.

An *advertising salesman* introduced several of Chuck's measurement techniques and four months later received the largest commission check in his six-year history with the company. He came into Chuck's program with a goal to increase sales 13%, and 90 days later increased the goal to 47% and eventually achieved a 55% increase the first year.

A *small grocery store* improved its shelf stocking efficiency 25%, from 30 to 40 cases per man-hour, with the adoption of one simple measuring technique.

A *building supply company* reduced inventory from $290,000 to $165,000, freeing $115,000 in operating capital, and at the same time increased the company's ability to fill orders.

A *wholesale lumberyard* decreased the number of man-hours per invoice from 4 to 1.9 for an annual savings of $147,000.

A *materials handling equipment company* reduced the number of days to process an invoice from 22 to 4.5 with the adoption of one simple measuring technique, resulting in a dramatic reduction in outstanding accounts receivable.

A *communications firm* realized a $3.4 million profit the first year after Chuck applied his measurement expertise. The year before, the company had realized a $1.7 million profit and had never realized more than a $2 million annual profit.

A *trucking company* reduced maintenance costs by $125,000 a year by charting an item as simple as the number of miles between breakdowns.

As you turn the pages in this book you will discover Chuck Coonradt's measurement philosophy upon which he built Western Leadership Group--a philosophy that has aided many companies and individuals in saving and earning millions of dollars. He calls it *The Game of Work.* He discusses key function indicators, Results to Resource Ratios, Fields of Play, scorecards and other terms which will help the reader understand as never before the elements of successful management by measurement—the kind of management that brings about astonishing results, cost savings and increased profits.

This book uncovers and explains in simple English some of the most profound principles of success and motivation ever contemplated by man. It uncovers the secrets of motivation in recreation and sports, and shows how those principles can be applied to business. It shows the reader the step by step method of accomplishing amazing results, with dozens of examples of how these principles can be implemented to achieve the kind of results mentioned earlier.

My experience with the pop bottles is only the tip of an iceberg, just an introduction to the management by measurement principles discussed in this book.

# The Slight Edge

On the locker room wall at Michigan State University there used to be a sign that said, "The difference between good and great is a little extra effort." The word "little" was italicized and emphasized. After many years the true significance of that statement is just beginning to sink in.

Rewards usually don't accurately represent the "little" differences between winners and those who finish second. Each year in the PGA golf tournament the winners are ranked by total earnings. In 1978 Tom Watson finished first, winning a total of $362,000, and was named the tour player of the year. Lee Trevino played in the same tournaments with the same equipment and won $224,000.

Is there a difference between Watson and Trevino? One earned $138,000 more than the other. But what about the difference in their play? Is Watson really 50% better than Trevino?

The PGA keeps track of the average strokes per round for all the tournament players. The final statistics show that in winning his $365,000 Tom Watson averaged 70.16 strokes for every eighteen holes of golf he played on the tour. Lee Trevino averaged 70.32. That's right! Sixteen hundredths, or one–sixth of a stroke, cost Lee Trevino $140,000 in winnings! Sixteen hundredths of a stroke, the difference between good and great, the little extra effort.

In 1982 Craig Stadler was the top money winner in the PGA with an average score of 70.71, earning $446,462. Number 20 that year was Johnny Miller, averaging 70.79 and earning $169,005. Stadler earned almost three times as much as Miller, while averaging only eight hundredths of a percentage point better per round!

15

That's what the slight edge is all about.

In 1982 the Indianapolis 500 was won by Gordon Johncock. It was the second closest finish in Indianapolis history. The margin of victory was 0.16 seconds in the three–hour road race. The estimated payoff to Johncock, including lap money and endorsements, was 12 times that of the driver who finished second. Do you remember who he was? Neither do I.

In 1981 the University of Utah ski team won the 1500 meter race by six centimeters in winning the NCAA national ski championship.

And talk of obscure second place finishes. Do you remember Mark Spitz, who won seven gold medals in the Munich Olympics in 1972? It was the most outstanding performance by an amateur athlete in the history of the games. Mark Spitz's largest winning margin to gain worldwide acclaim and attention was less than two full seconds. Can you remember any of the swimmers who finished second behind Spitz? Truly the difference between good and great is a little extra effort.

The famous 1981 Belmont Stakes race between Affirmed and Alydar was so close that it took the steward 20 minutes to determine that Affirmed had won the race—the fourth horse in history to win racing's Triple Crown. The payoff and the fame difference between those two horses is incalculable. And so it goes throughout every field of endeavor, even the company where you work.

As you look for winners in your company, as you seek to establish a winning environment, think about the difference between winners and losers in baseball. A .200 hitter is moved about by managers like they change their socks. A .300 hitter like Reggie Jackson is so valuable that when he fights with his manager you can guess who they fire!

The difference between a .300 hitter and a .200 hitter is one more hit in every ten trips to the plate. If you take the full count, it's one more hit in every 60 pitches.

That same seemingly small margin in business makes a difference too. One more start in every 60 days. One more effective phone call in every 60 that we make. One more effective contact in every 60 employees we talk to. One more effective minute in every 60 minutes we work. This book will help you build that slight edge for success.

If you haven't looked at yourself as a sports entity before, it's time you did. You really are like an athlete in that you have certain talents, abilities and energy which you market for money and recognition. You are a participant in *The Game of Work,* whether you like it or not, and this book is not only about making the cut, but becoming a superstar.

You are also the coach of your own team, and you alone are responsible for developing your abilities and talents so you can market them for more money. In addition to being responsible for your own growth and development, there may be others whose productivity you are responsible for. If so, the principles discussed in this book are even more important to you. You are a coach as well as a player. Think sports and how the motivational principles of athletics can apply to your business, and you will have a slight edge as you read this book.

In business, the person earning $60,000 a year is *not* three times better than the person earning $20,000 a year. He just has a slight edge. He does a few things better. Often the slight edge is nothing more than a better understanding of scorekeeping, or self–motivation.

As you read these pages, keep in mind that this book is an investment in your future. The principles presented in the following pages can work for you as they have worked for hundreds of thousands of other people.

But before you go any further, get out of your chair, walk into the bathroom, and look at yourself in the mirror. Say, "I am a player." Say it a couple of times. Set your mind to the idea that you are a true competitor. You may not be competing in the NBA, NFL or LPGA, but you are competing in your own game of life in a very real way––a way that is very similar to athletic competition.

Go ahead, do it. It's the first step in converting your work into a game, complete with scorecards, batting averages, and shooting percentages.

### Your Scouting Report

The Dallas Cowboys have been in the playoffs more than any other team in the NFL. One of the keys to their success is the elaborate scouting reports they maintain on not only professional and college athletes, but high school players as well.

Let's discuss you, your talents and abilities. Let's build a scouting report. In the space below, list the talents and abilities you market for money. List the most important ones first.

1.
2.
3.
4.
5.

Now list the things you have done over the years to improve your talents and abilities. Include schooling, seminars, subscriptions to trade journals, etc. Beside each list the approximate cost.

1. College                                Cost:
2. Post Graduate Studies       Cost:
3. Seminars & Workshops       Cost:
4. Books                             Cost:
5. Trade Journals                Cost:
6. Other _____   Cost:
    _____   Cost:
    _____   Cost:

Your training may have covered:

(1) *Know–how or skills*, what you have learned to do.

(2) *Energy*, your ability to roll up your sleeves and keep your nose to the grindstone day after day.

(3) *Time*, not how much you have, but how you organize your time and make it work for you.

(4) *Imagination*, that creative spark, coming up with the ideas nobody else thought of.

(5) *Planning and goal setting*, how well you set goals and develop workable plans to achieve those goals.

(6) *Communications skills*, how well you present your ideas and suggestions to others so they are willing to accept and carry out your suggestions.

(7) *Decision–making ability*, how well you gather and assimilate facts to make good decisions.

If you had a magic wand and could have any one of these talents or abilities in rich abundance, which would it be? Which one, if developed to perfection, would be most useful to you? Of course, you would probably like to see your abilities in all of the above categories improved, but there is probably one area where you need the most help right now. Which is it?

Write it down here:

Albert Einstein said he developed about 10% of his potential. What would you guess is your percentage of developed potential **right now?**

You see, there is plenty of room for improvement. What seminars or classes could you take to improve the above talent or ability? How much would that cost in time and money?

You know how much you have invested in this book, and that is only a fraction of what a reputable seminar or college course would cost, yet the principles presented in this book have brought immediate and remarkable improvement to thousands of people. They have worked for others, and they will work for you if you go about it right.

## Goals

The principles in this book will help you reach your most desired goals. You have heard of goals and have some, I hope. If not, here's something you must consider. All organizations rise or fall on the personal goals of the individuals in that organization.

Only 3% of Americans are independently wealthy; they can live off the income from their investment capital.

The next 10% live comfortably, the way most of us would like to live.

And 60% barely make a living, from one paycheck to the next.

The last 27% need support from others or the government just to survive.

What is the difference between these three groups? Leadership Management, Inc. (LMI) has consistently found that the top 3% have written, specific goals. They keep score. The 10% level have goals generally in mind, but they are not *specific and written*.

Obviously, the achievement of goals involves a lot more than just writing down goals. Otherwise there would be a lot more than 3% in that top group.

## Success/Results

Paul J. Meyer, president of S.M.I. International, says success is the progressive realization of worthwhile predetermined personal goals. Napoleon Hill said that success is the pursuit of a worthy ideal. Success is results. That's what we're in business for. In sports, success is measured in touchdowns, the Lombardi Trophy, winning the Super Bowl, the NBA title or the Stanley Cup. If you ask yourself what the key ingredient to success is, you come up with the word *behavior*.

## Behavior/Success/Results

You cannot change the result without changing the behavior. That's a frightening lesson for many of us to learn, but a true one. I cannot get consequence B by behaving in way A. "I would like to lose weight as long as I don't have to give up the hot fudge." "I want to be financially independent but I can't give up my credit cards." "I'd like to be a marathon runner, but don't ask me to run in the rain." "I'd like to compete in downhill skiing, but I don't want to take lessons."

There's no way to get around the fact that behavior precedes results. As the behavior of players determines the team results, so does the behavior of workers and managers determine the success of a business. Too often businesses try to blame outside influences if they don't get desired results, when it's the way the players behave that determines whether or not the team wins with any degree of consistency.

We can go one step further. Attitude is the prime cause of behavior.

## Attitude/Behavior/Success/Results

The way I *think* determines the way I will *act*, whether it be momentary in a fit of rage or contemplative in a planning session. It is imperative to understand that the thought must precede the act. Also, it is impossible to behave consistently contrary to a value–held attitude, maybe temporarily by coercion, force or inducement, but not consistently.

This brings us to a dilemma facing every coach. He may be able to specify what behavior is required in a player to produce the desired result, but he doesn't know how to mold the attitude so the desired behavior can be achieved.

There are two powerful forces which form attitudes. One is a significant emotional event (SEE). The death of a loved one while participating in a sport may significantly shape our attitude towards that sport. A severe reprimand from the first boss may shape a worker's attitude towards management for years to come. Significant emotional events, while necessary and recognized attitude modifiers, are not easily duplicated in coaching environments. They are difficult to control.

The second formative force in attitude is conditioning. Conditioning is the same force that trains the dog with the electric collar, or Pavlov's dog, to ring the bell or salivate.

You may say you don't have an electric collar, but you must

admit that your past conditioning influences the way you act. We have all been raised with the statements:

"Children should be seen and not heard."

"Never bite off more than you can chew."

"Never speak unless spoken to."

"Never go where you're not wanted."

"Never get in the car with a stranger."

"Never take candy from a stranger."

"Never talk to strangers."

If you're in a marketing role, your entire job description is contrary to the great motherly advice that kept you safely out of the clutches of kidnappers on your way to school. The cornerstone of sales–call reluctance in the American sales force was planted there on those sidewalks to kindergarten.

If you don't believe me, walk into the nearest elevator and recognize that it's a six– by eight–foot American institution where 14 strangers can stand close enough to touch each other and nobody talks. We all duck in, turn around and look at the numbers above the door.

The next time you get into an elevator, do not turn around. Simply face your fellow passengers. Watch their eyes go to the floor. And if you feel bold, say,

"Good morning, how are you?"

You can't tell me conditioning does not shape attitudes.

## Conditioning/Attitudes/Behavior/Success/Results

What makes conditioning such a powerful force? Repetition. Spaced repetition. We did not learn to avoid strangers because we were told once, but because most of us were told every time we left the house to be wary of strangers. Perhaps all of our mothers went to school together and learned to say the same things to their children. None of us were brash enough to turn aound as we left the house and wonder what our other choices were. It didn't occur to us to question the source of that information. But today how many of our investment philosophies, or management decisions, are guided by those youthful admonitions?

Today, how many of us "look before we leap," "save our money for a rainy day," and "make sure that if we can't say something nice about somebody we don't say anything at all?" This last one has had a great impact on restricting management discipline.

When you are coaching you must understand that success is the result of behavior, which is determined by attitudes, which are formed by conditioning, which takes place through spaced repetition.

Repetitive learning is the only vehicle to modify conditioning, which alters the attitudes that control our behavior, which produces the results we want. One trip, one lecture, one seminar, one tape won't do it. Advertisers say it takes eight repetitions before the consumer will even notice your product.

Winners understand the importance of conditioning as it relates to attitudes, behavior and eventually achieving success or results. Winners are constantly conditioning themselves by reviewing their written goals, reading good books, surrounding themselves with other goal–oriented individuals, and inviting spaced repetition of positive thoughts while pushing negative thoughts out of their minds.

You can bet the Washington Redskins don't make up very many plays during the course of a game. The bread and butter plays of their offense have been rehearsed in practice dozens, if not hundreds, of times. The players are conditioned by repetition to respond in a predetermined way to each play number.

Winners in business also understand the conditioning process, the need for spaced repetition, and do everything in their power to utilize this powerful force in achieving success and results.

**Spaced Repetition**

The reason expensive seminars and workshops generally work better than self–improvement books is spaced repetition, the learning technique that turns good ideas into behavior traits. A quick reading of a good book might yield one or two good ideas, but they are usually forgotten.

Which national advertising do you remember best? Those with spaced repetitions, of course. Think of words like Camaro, Crest, and Marlboro.

Have you ever listened to a motivational speaker who impressed you with his message, but a week later you could remember very little and had applied nothing from the speech?

That's exactly what happens to ideas without spaced repetition. My experience with S.M.I. International, Inc. has convinced me that as much as 60% of an idea is accepted only after six repetitions. Have you ever read a self–help book more than once? More than twice? Yet, for 60% of the message of a book to become part of you, you would have to read it at least six times!

Without spaced repetition this book will be just another interesting reading experience with very little actually adopted by you to improve your talents and abilities and your managment effectiveness.

Therefore, if you want this book to go to work for you, to help you achieve dramatic improvements in your talents and abilities, you need to do more than just one quick reading, although you should start with that. You need to be convinced that the principles in this book can do for you what Lee Nelson said in the foreward that they did for him.

Read the entire book cover to cover, underlining key points, then go back for the spaced repetitions. Read the first chapter every night or every morning for an entire week. You'll find yourself thinking about the concepts presented there on the way to work, during your lunch hours, even in your dreams. During working hours, you'll be on the lookout to apply the principles in the first chapter. By the end of the week, the first chapter will be a part of your thinking and actions. The second week, take the second chapter and do the same: read it once each day and make it a part of your daily life. After eleven weeks and eleven chapters you will see marked improvement in your abilities and productivity--as much improvement as if you had paid thousands of dollars to attend the most expensive seminars in the world.

Try to get friends or work associates to go through the book with you, a chapter at a time, week by week. Then discuss daily the principles and their possible applications, perhaps over lunch. The results will be even more dramatic. You will come away from this book with a plan of action for a more productive and happy life. You will go to bed at night one of the few people in the world who know exactly where you are going, how you are going to get there, and knowing it is only a matter of time until you achieve your goals. You will have the slight edge.

# The Game of Work

*People will pay for the privilege of working harder than they will work when they are paid.*

--Chuck Coonradt

Consider the frozen food business where people are hired to work in refrigerated warehouses. Terrible working conditions at near zero temperatures. But the unions and OSHA have done much to make conditions bearable. Companies are required to provide insulated clothing and boots. In fact, an entire industry provides refrigiwear clothing to companies with refrigerated warehouses. These companies are required to provide hot drinks within so many feet of cold work areas. Workers must have a 10-minute break every hour. It's tough to get people to work in those kinds of conditions. People dislike working in the cold.

Yet, whenever a winter snowstorm passes over my home in the mountains near Salt Lake City, followed by clearing skies and plunging temperatures, there is a sudden jump in employee absenteeism, particularly among young workers. Instead of staying home to avoid contact with freezing temperatures, they migrate up the local canyons to test the new and famous powder snow at Alta, Snowbird or Park City.

Equipped with hundreds of dollars' worth of equipment, they gladly take a reduction in pay for the day off and buy a $20 pass to spend the day outside in sub-freezing temperatures. There are no hot drink vending machines on the slopes, nor have I ever heard of a skier demanding a 10-minute break every hour. People really will pay for the privilege of working harder than they will work when they are paid.

Consider deer hunting. Every year during the third week in October, hundreds of thousands of men drag themselves to work Monday through Thursday. They are slow, lethargic, saving energy for the weekend. Then on Thursday afternoon it's as if every one of them takes some kind of magic energy pill. Their eyes open wide. They stay up all night cleaning rifles, sharpening knives, waterproofing boots and loading the camper with hundreds of dollars' worth of food. The next day they spend five or six hours driving along the roughest roads in the world, often in snowstorms. The next morning--the same men who on work days have trouble fixing a bowl of cold cereal--are up at 4 a.m. fixing a huge breakfast of bacon, eggs, fried potatoes, juice, and hot drinks.

After breakfast they wander out into a freezing blizzard, hoping for a chance to drag a dead deer through places they wouldn't carry their dying mother--all the time pretending the deer meat they might get is an economical investment to cut future grocery bills. Those hunters pay for the privilege of working harder than they will work when they are paid.

But why? Why do people put up to ten times as much energy and effort into their avocation as into their vocation? Why will people pay for the privilege of working harder than they will work when they are paid?

**First. In recreation goals are more clearly defined.** Shooting a deer. Winning a game. Beating your previous time. The desired result is clear and easily measured.

I've always wanted to golf at Pebble Beach in Carmel, California. That's where they hold the annual Bing Crosby Pro–Am tournament. I'd love to play Pebble Beach.

Let's assume I finally make it to the course.

"I'm here to play," I say. "Where is a map of the course?"

"We don't have a map of the course anymore," says the guy at the door.

"How do I know where to play? Where's the first green?" I ask.

"Well, we changed," the guy says. "With property values so high we have converted half the course into condos. As a result we've changed the rules some. There's no longer a first tee."

"Well, do you have a second tee?"

"We don't have a second tee, either. In fact, we don't have any tees anymore."

"Uh, well. What about the greens?"

"Don't have those either."

"Are the boundaries gone too?"

"Yes, except that it's off limits to hit a ball in somebody's yard."

"How do I play?"

"Well," he says. "We've analyzed why people play golf, and the big reason is exercise. Here's a pedometer. Go out and walk 6700 yards, wherever you wish. You won't need a caddy because you only need to take along one club. Stop and swing it whenever you wish, a minimum of 70 times or until you feel like you've had the normal amount of exercise for an 18–hole game of golf."

"You're kidding!" I say.

"But the best part of the game hasn't changed," he continues. "When you're finished walking and swinging you can still come back to the bar and talk about the shots you almost made. And if you want to bet on your game...."

Can you imagine going out on the soccer field and someone saying, "Listen, you guys. Mostly this game is running and exercise. We don't want to do all the accounting, so we just took the goals out. You can run around kicking the ball for 45 minutes, then we'll take a break. Then you can run around another 45 minutes. You can go home and tell everyone how well you exercised."

No fun. Right? How hard do you think it would be to fill the stadium for the soccer world cup if there were no goals?

In recreation goals are more clearly defined than in business. Without goals recreation would be meaningless. If you took the goals out of football you would have to give the Lombardi Trophy to the team that racked up the most yards. If you took the yard-markers away you would have to give the Lombardi Trophy to the team that stayed on the field the longest, just like we do in business!

If you took the measurements out of the New York Marathon there is no way in the world you'd ever get 40,000 people to stand and wait two hours on the Brooklyn Bridge in the pre–dawn hours for a chance to run 26 miles.

**Second. In recreation the scorekeeping is better**, because it's more objective, self–administered, and peer audited.

I play golf with an 18 handicap, and I will pull out my checkbook and play golf with anybody who will accept that. If I break 85 on 18 holes I'm in heaven. But sometimes I play with guys with eight or ten handicaps. If they hit 85, they are going the other way and I take their money.

In golf you get realistic feedback that you can relate to your own past performance. If you were getting feedback comparing you to Jack Nicklaus you would soon become discouraged and quit because you could never win. But accurate feedback related to your own past performance usually gives you enough positive reinforcement to want to keep playing, to keep improving, to beat your own past performance standards. You win frequently enough to want to keep playing.

Have you ever met a runner who couldn't tell you how fast he runs his miles? Anybody can be a jogger—just shuffle along and you've got it. But a runner must run miles in less than eight minutes. Every serious runner keeps score. If you consistently run eight-minute miles, then you really feel good about yourself if you finish a workout averaging 7:40 miles. And if you break seven, that's all you can talk about all day. You don't feel bad because you didn't break the four-minute mile, or because you are not running marathons in two hours. You feel great because you are measuring yourself against your own past performance and winning. If you ran your last marathon in 4:10, then you feel great when you break four hours. You don't feel let down if you didn't make 2:40. You feel like a winner because you are not comparing your performance to some unrealistic standard.

In recreation everybody knows how to keep score. In business, however, sometimes the strokes don't count. Sometimes nobody cares. Frequently workers don't understand the scorekeeping system. Frequently there is too little objectivity in business scorekeeping.

There's a tennis tournament, sponsored by a local television station in Salt Lake City every summer, that draws 2,700 participants with only four people keeping score. In a professional golf tournament with 140 participants, there are three people keeping score and they sit in a tent and never see a stroke. Why? Because the scorecards are self-administered and peer audited.

If you turned a golf tournament over to the American Management Association they'd assign 200 supervisors. If you gave the contract to a computer company you'd have so much cable lying on the course you couldn't find the balls.

In recreation the scorekeeping enables you to receive immediate and realistic feedback. You know at all times how you are doing.

Assume you are on the golf course playing for $20 a hole and you're standing on the seventeenth hole. You have two holes left to play and you're behind, so you talk your opponent into pressing the bet--double the bet on the last two holes in an effort to catch up.

You step up to the tee and blast the ball over the fence. You don't have to wait until the next six-month interview with the golf pro to know you blew it. You have been keeping your own score on every hole and know exactly where you stand.

You feel badly, not because you didn't play as well as Jack Nicklaus, but because you didn't play up to your personal expectations corresponding to your handicap.

Scorekeeping is an effective form of motivation if it is objective, self-administered and peer audited.

### Third. In recreation feedback is more frequent.

I believe that everybody needs to know every day whether he or she is winning or losing. What do you think would happen if the commissioner of pro football walked onto the field at the beginning of the annual Super Bowl game to determine the best football team in the world, and said to the players,

"Guys, we're going to be more businesslike in our approach to football today. We're not going to keep score. The commissioners are just going to watch the game, then meet and decide which team played the best. We'll let you know what we decide within three months." The commissioner would have to run for his life!

Fortunately, in most recreational activities you don't have to depend on a boss or supervisor to tell you how you are doing. You know what the score is as the game progresses, and nobody can change that just because they don't like you. The feedback is accurate and frequent--you know where you stand every time you throw the ball. And everybody knows how to keep score.

Feedback is the breakfast of champions. People who want to get ahead, who want to win, who want to improve and get the job done--these people want feedback.

If you want to improve the quality of performance in any area you simply improve or increase the frequency of feedback. If you have a problem and you are getting a quarterly report, change it to a monthly report. If that doesn't do the job turn it into a weekly or daily report. By increasing the frequency you have more opportunities to catch and eliminate problems of a solvable size.

### Fourth. In recreation participants feel they have a higher degree of choice.

Think about the words that imply a lack of choice--words frequently used in business. Words like "have to," "gotta," "oughta," "should," "must." How many times have you heard someone say "gotta go play tennis"?

I'm a tennis player and I don't have much respect for golfers. They don't get any exercise. They hit the ball, get in the cart, hit the ball again and get back in the cart.

I know some racquetballers who don't have much respect for us tennis players. They think we go out to get our legs tanned. Then there's the handball players who say real men don't need racquets. Part of the reason for liking a recreational activity is the free choice you enjoy in choosing to do it.

Managers must ask themselves if they are utilizing the principle of choice when giving out assignments to employees. Are people being allowed to perform in areas where they have natural interests and abilities, or is it like the Army with the bakers being ordered to drive trucks? When people feel like they have no choice in what they are doing they lose enthusiasm, and performance suffers.

**Fifth. In recreation they don't change the rules in the middle of the game.**

Assume you are playing pool in a strange town and winning. You just put in the eighth ball when somebody announces that it didn't count because you didn't say "Molly Mumford" before it went in the hole. Obviously, you are upset because someone changed the rules on you. That doesn't happen in sports. If the basketball goes through the hoop you get two points. The pros and some college leagues have three–point baskets, but the rules for getting three–point baskets are set up during the off season, never in the middle of a game. In business, however, rules are frequently changed in the middle of the game.

One time I sat down with a regional sales manager for a light bulb manufacturer. We were talking about scorekeeping and maintaining a high motivational level among the salespeople.

"We have a good scorekeeping system," he said. "Our people get regular reports listing their point accumulations, yet the system doesn't seem to motivate our people."

"That sounds strange," I said, because at first appearance it looked like a good scorekeeping system.

Then he said, "I guess the thing they are upset about is the Annual National Quota Adjustment."

"What?" I said.

"Annual National Quota Adjustment," he repeated matter–of–factly, like I ought to be familiar with the term.

"Tell me about it," I said.

"If the whole company," he explained, "does 125% of quota, then we depreciate the value of everybody's points back down to the 100% level."

"It's obvious to me," I said, "that your people can't count on a stroke being a stroke. You are changing the rules in the middle of the game."

Consider a grocery store situation where the meat manager has just been chewed out by the store manager for not making enough money on his meat.

"We're going to fix this," says the store manager to the meat manager. "We're going to pinch every nickel and dime in this department and we are going to start making some money!" The meat manager nods his agreement.

Mrs. Jones comes in the store an hour later with a bad ham. She goes back to the meat manager, who has just had the rules laid down to him about watching the nickels and dimes. He gives her a hard time about exchanging the ham. She gives up and goes to the store manager, who says,

"No problem, Mrs. Jones. I'll take you back and explain to that stupid meat manager of mine how we are going to have customer satisfaction around here." The manager has changed the rules in the middle of the game.

Now, if they changed the rules in a football game, the referee saying after a touchdown that the ball carrier got into the end zone too easily, that the touchdown would only be worth four points, what do you think would happen?

Changing the rules in the middle of the game adds to the uncertainty of the game. Good managers seek to minimize uncertainty. Workers, like athletes, perform better when they know where they stand, when they know the score. A feeling of certainty creates a sense of security and a warm feeling about working conditions. A manager cannot eliminate all uncertainty, but by avoiding changing the rules in the middle of the game he can go a long way towards minimizing uncertainty.

In the workplace, when expectations are clearly defined and uncertainty is minimized, it is easier for people to realize the satisfaction of meeting expectations.

What do you think would happen if these five principles could be applied in the working world? If work could be turned into a game? If people applied themselves as diligently in work as in recreational pursuits? That is what this book is all about. That is why it is called *The Game of Work*.

There's a productivity crisis in America. We hear about it

every day. Yet while our workers become less competitive or productive, recreational interests and abilities are growing by leaps and bounds.

If the office air conditioning goes off on a hot day, and if it's a 100 degrees outside, soon the temperature of the office gets up to about 80 degrees. People start tugging at their shirts, saying, "Boy, it's tough working in here. We better go home early."

We all agree that it's tough to work when the temperature gets up to 80 degrees. But the minute we step outside where it's 100 degrees, somebody says,

"What do you think, golf or tennis?"

The principles that lead to motivation in recreation can be applied to business with remarkable results. In this book we will uncover and define those principles, then teach you how to apply them.

When people receive the same positive feedback at work that they get in their favorite recreational pursuit, they show more interest in the work, more even than in recreation, because they are getting paid for their work. Professional athletes get paid to play. Resolve today to become a pro.

# Goals

*In the absence of clearly defined goals, we are forced to concentrate on activity and ultimately become enslaved by it.*

*--Chuck Coonradt*

Let's take a look at what goal setting does in athletics. If you took the goals out of football, what would you have? You would give the Lombardi Trophy to the team each year that racked up the most yardage--and if you took the yard markers off the field you would have to give it to the team that could stay on the field the longest. Then football would be like many businesses that use longevity as the main criteria for promoting some managers.

If you took the goals out of basketball, you would have ten guys running up and down the floor just dribbling the ball--like we do in business sometimes, even without the ball.

If you took the goals out of hockey, you would have 12 guys on the ice fighting, and some people think that would improve the sport. Everything we do in our recreational pursuits is absolutely and totally goal directed. In hunting we have the Boone and Crockett Club to record the largest, widest and best antler spread, and the highest quality trophies taken. Thousands of man-hours a week are spent updating the NFL record book.

If you took the goals out of any sport, you would remove the most significant aspect of recreational pursuit--goal setting and striving. There is something inherent in us to want to do it better, faster, higher, shorter, longer, and to win.

When John Nabors set up a three–year training program in 1973 after seeing Mark Spitz win his gold medals in the previous Olympics, John didn't just want to become a good swimmer. He didn't just climb in the pool and swim his heart out twice a day for 165 weeks for the fun of it. He didn't do it because it was great exercise. He did it because he had a specific goal to become the best in the world at his event.

Goals are the motivating force in athletics. And in athletics, goals are more clearly defined than in business. Goals are the main reason people will pay for the privilege of working harder than they will work when they are paid.

When we walk onto the tennis court, we know the goal is to win. When we go onto a football or soccer field we know where we have to put ourselves, and what our performance has to be to score. We must have that same challenge, that same opportunity, that same motivation, when we walk into the office in the morning––instead of waiting for the phone to ring or the mail to hit the desk to get things happening.

Goals in recreation are clearly defined, and as a result motivation in recreation is at a higher level than in business. Can we bring the motivation of recreation into the workplace? Absolutely!

When the following criteria for goal setting are applied in the workplace they can produce motivation similar to that found in recreation.

### 1. Goals must be written.

One of the reasons Don Schula took his Miami Dolphins to the 1983 Super Bowl following the 1982 strike–plagued season is that every week they prepared to play. Every week their goals were in writing, well–organized, specific.

People will avoid the written goals process and say, "I don't need to know that. I can keep my important goals in my head. I can concentrate on the things that are really meaningful in my life." And then if the phone rings in the middle of that conversation and their spouse is on the other end asking them to pick up five items from the grocery store, they say, "Hold it. Let me get a pencil and a piece of paper so I won't forget."

Goals that are not written are merely wishes. There is something in the act of writing a goal down that makes it real, gives it permanence, removes it from the realm of fleeting whims. Goals that are not written down are easily forgotten or changed;

written goals that are reviewed regularly become reality. Unwritten goals cannot be read and reviewed. When goals are not written, the power of conditioning through spaced repetition is lost.

I am continuously amazed how people, after paying huge tuitions to attend seminars, resist and even fight the concept of written goals. They must think the Dallas Cowboys make up their plays during their games. Ridiculous. The main difference between professional and sandlot football is the amount of written documentation of the goals program.

A team's goal is not just to win the championship or to be the best. A good goals program is detailed and specific—yards per carry, number of offensive and defensive plays, plays per series. Goals must be broken down into a specific plan, in writing.

It is impossible to manage successful lives in violation of the principle of written goal setting. None of us would build a $200,000 house without a set of plans from the architect. But the average income earner producing $20,000 a year for ten years ($200,000), will spend it without a goals program, without a set of plans, then wonder at the end of the ten–year period why he has nothing more than the appreciation on his house. Goals must be written.

## 2. Goals must be your own.

Super Bowl rings are won by individual players. The greatest successes in sports are the result of individual commitments to personal success.

Franz Klammer, the Austrian downhiller who roared to victory in the giant slalom in the 1980 Winter Olympics on his home course, needed to better his best time by .3 seconds to win. In downhill skiing, .3 seconds is a huge margin. Klammer was the last one down the course that day. It was covered with icy ruts from the earlier skiers and the fog had moved in, making it impossible for a skier to see more than two flags at one time.

Later, Klammer said, "When I left the gate, I decided that I would win or die." He won.

I remember game seven of the 1977 World Series. The Yankees were playing the Dodgers in Yankee Stadium. Up until that game Reggie Jackson was not having a great series. He was catching a lot of flak in the New York press. In game seven he hit three home runs, leading the Yankees to victory. Why did Reggie do so well? For his team? Possibly. For George Steinbrenner? Certainly not. He did it for Reggie Jackson.

Whose company do you work for? Mine. Whose boss do I work for? Mine. Whose income am I most concerned about? Mine.

I, me, my, mine. Whose goals are the most important to me? Mine.

You no doubt have observed people who go through life giving just the minimum daily requirement at work, and yet when the whistle sounds, they are off to coach a Little League team, play in a bowling league, build a mountain cabin—do something that is uniquely theirs. You've noticed the transformation, the new energy, the intelligence, the creativity, the endurance and capacity for work. Awesome.

Goal setting and striving becomes truly effective only when team or corporate goals become synonymous with personal goals. When it becomes my team or my company. If you look at the employees of the finest organizations, the ones that we admire, they talk about "my company." These employees have entrepreneural instincts to help ensure the success of their companies because their own personal goals are intertwined with the company goals.

### 3. Goals must be positive.

Vince Lombardi said that the objective of the game is to win—fairly, squarely and by the rules, but to win. The goal in sports is not to avoid a loss or defeat. How many times have you seen a PGA golfer going down the stretch, changing his game plan to protect his lead instead of going for everything he can get, only to see his lead slip away? He gets beaten because he loses the momentum of his earlier positive attack.

The batting average is an excellent example of a positive goal. Consider George Brett, who has had the highest season average in modern times, or Rod Carew, who has won more batting titles than any other player in the recent history of the game. Neither has been able to bat above the mystical .400 mark, the goal set by Ted Williams but never achieved. We consider the .400 average a positive goal. We don't look at that magical mark as being wrong 60 percent of the time. In baseball we keep track of hits and home runs, not strike outs.

The two most common goals in America are to quit smoking and to lose weight—both negative. I used to smoke—and talk about a habit reinforced by spaced repetition. A pack a day, 365 days a year—7,300 times a year, reaching for the smokes. The problem is getting your arm to quit moving from pocket to mouth.

Rather than have the negative goal to quit smoking, someone who wants to stop must have a goal to become a non-smoker. Non-smokers have tremendous benefits. They get lower rates on life and car insurance. Their clothes last longer. They don't ruin furniture or carpets. Their smell is not offensive to others. They are non–smokers, a positive thing to be.

The problem is that most people who quit still see themselves as smokers on vacation or on the wagon, and it is just a matter of time until they start up again.

I once had a young man in my course who told me he smoked between a pack and a half and two packs of cigarettes a day. When I said, "Oh, 35 cigarettes a day," he looked at me and said, "Oh no. It couldn't possibly be that many." But as you work the numbers out, a pack and a half is 30, two packs is 40, and somewhere between the two is 35.

As he began to clearly identify the magnitude of his habit, he then started graphing and tracking his progress to smoke a predetermined number of cigarettes a day.

The first day, I suggested that he smoke 35, his average in the past and something that wouldn't present any challenge. He called me at 10:00 that night asking, "Do I have to smoke all 35? I'm up to 32 and frankly, I've had enough." To make him successful in his attempt to reach a predetermined goal, I insisted he smoke all 35, which he did.

The next day he set a goal of 34 cigarettes. Now you might say, "Ah, clever, you're asking him to cut back a cigarette a day." No, I'm asking him to smoke a predetermined number of cigarettes each day so he can get it in his mind that he can determine in his own mind how many he will smoke every day. With that positive attitude and conditioning, his goal went to 32 a day, 31, and 30.

After two weeks he said he wanted to quit, but I said no because I figured he needed more reinforcement before he stopped something he had been doing almost 7,000 times a year for many years. Every morning as he decided how many cigarettes and at which times he would smoke, he always kept the after dinner smoke at the end of his list. He learned to smoke as many cigarettes as he decided each morning. When his goal finally was to smoke zero cigarettes a day, he could truly in his own mind say, "I am a non–smoker."

The same principle applies to losing weight. Imagine losing 20 pounds. What are you going to do? Cut off an arm? Sometimes many of us feel that would be less painful than the way we go about it. Instead of a negative goal in pounds that need to be lost, the goal must be to achieve an optimal weight, and to maintain that weight once it is achieved.

The problem with people losing weight is that after they take it off they go out and celebrate and stuff it back on again with hot fudge sundaes and lemon meringue pies––at least those are my favorites. You must be able to visualize the goal, and the only way the goal can be visual is if it is positive.

In basketball and football they count the points you score, not the ones you miss. But in life many times we will do 80% of the task and then when asked to report on it say, "Nope, I failed."

We must be willing, as the song says,

To accentuate the positive
And eliminate the negative.
Latch onto the affirmative
And don't mess with Mr. In-Between.

Your mind rejects negative goals; they are hard to visualize.

## 4. Goals must be measurable and specific.

In sports we demand numbers—two, three and even four places to the right of the decimal point. Strokes in golf are no longer a small enough measurement. It's hundredths of strokes that count. The times of swimmers, speed skaters and downhill skiers are all measured in thousandths of seconds, and in order to separate one athlete from the others these kinds of exact measurements are essential.

How much, how many, and by when? If you can't measure it, how will you know when you achieved it? Even intangible goals need tangible indicators. If you have a goal to be more patient, count how many times you beat your kids in a month, or how many times you raise your voice. If the numbers drop, your patience is increasing. Don't say, "I am going to be a better salesman next year," but "I am going to make X number of calls next year."

S.M.I. president Paul Meyer, the world's leading authority on goal setting, insists, "Definite goals produce definite results. On the other hand, indefinite goals do not produce indefinite results. They produce no results at all."

If you put 100 people in a room and ask them all how many would like to be financially independent, all the hands go up. If you then come back and ask how many have a current personal financial statement detailing his or her assets, liabilities and net worth that is current in the last 90 days—and I don't mean the paper you had to fill out to get a loan at the bank—90 of those 100 people will not raise their hands.

If you continue your questioning of those remaining 10 people and say, "Now, how many have that financial statement laid out in a pro-forma goals format for one, three, five, ten and twenty year periods?" Nine of them are going to sit down and the one that is still standing is the millionaire. It doesn't make any difference what his background is, how much money he has, or what his current income earning position is. That individual has a plan, and with that plan you cannot turn him aside. Goals must answer the question how much, how many and by when.

If our company philosophy claims the customer to be king, then we may want to measure the percentage of orders coming from repeat customers, the size of orders per customer, or the number of complaints per thousand transactions and how we dealt with them. Unless the overall goals of the company reflect how much, how many, by when and by whom, we really don't have a legitimate goals program.

## 5. Goals are best stated in inflation-proof terms.

We've discussed the illusive goal of a .400 batting average—an inflation-proof goal that has not changed in 40 years since Ted Williams achieved it. Salaries and commissions may go up or down. Ticket prices may go up, but some things are always the same—minutes, hours, pounds, hits, baskets, touchdowns. Goals are best stated in units of measurements that don't change.

There is a paper company in the Northwest that decided to produce fine paper. They have been in the pulp business for many years, chopping up trees and making paper, and are accustomed to measuring production in tons, not dollars.

Back in the late '60s the fine paper division was established. They took a controller out of headquarters and sent him over to run the new division. He was a tonnage man, not a dollar man, when it came to measuring production.

He was told that in the fine paper industry, everything was measured in dollar value. He said, "Nope, we're going to count pounds and tons, even in the sales department."

About this time, a sudden paper shortage appeared worldwide, and paper prices went nuts. While everyone else was measuring dollar sales volumes and patting themselves on the backs with 13 and 14 percent sales increases each year when prices were going up 20 and 30 percent a year, the guys at this new fine paper division were hustling to beat pound quotas. While inflation lulled the bulk of the companies in the fine paper industry into a false sense of security, this company was capturing a huge share of the market. They'd set their goals in non-inflationary numbers.

The majority of retail stores in the United States today have not managed to have their sales per customer keep up with the increases in inflation. The actual tonnage or amount of product sold in these stores has actually decreased while dollar sales have increased. Most of them have actually been behind on the score board and didn't even know it, thanks to inflation and short-sighted management. Inflation is a fact. It can be good or bad, but it is a real force in business. Only when we can take it out of our goals program, as that paper company did, can we be the benefactors rather than the victims of inflation.

### 6. Goals must be stated in the most visible terms available.

When goals are measured in real things, everybody knows the score. There's no monkey business. When the points go up on an NFL scoreboard, everybody knows what is happening, who is ahead and who is catching up or widening their lead.

Goals should be measured in something you can see. Percentages are too vague. The salesman says to the sales manager that after a long period of thought and soul searching he has set a goal to increase his volume by 25 percent.

"Great," responds the sales manager. "According to my records, last January you achieved 10,000 unit sales. According to your goal you'll get 12,500 this January. Fantastic!"

"Wait a minute," says the salesman. "There's no way I'll get 12,500 in January, but the 25 percent increase will be a cinch."

Nonsense. He may have some nebulous feeling that somehow he'll make it up in December, but that won't happen if he is afraid in January to face his goal in real numbers. Even dollars are better than percentages. Goals must be stated in pounds, units, calls, boxes—things you can taste and touch.

Organizations can measure labor in at least four different ways:

a) *Labor costs in relation to dollar sales.* (Most accountants prefer this measurement.)

b) *Dollar sales per person–hour.*

c) *Invoices or customers served per person–hour.*

d) *Pounds or tons produced per person–hour.*

The cost of labor and dollar sales are both inflationary indicators and therefore can get very complicated and hard to figure. If wage costs and sales prices do not change in a parallel fashion, you end up comparing apples and oranges. In comparing labor costs to dollar sales you are using two variables, both of which are subject to inflationary changes. You are better off comparing dollar sales to person–hours where only the first variable is vulnerable to inflation changes. Hours are easy to measure because they are non–inflationary. There will never be more than 60 minutes in an hour. Other non–inflationary variable units include invoices, customers, pounds, tons, etc.

I once gave the following problem to a group of managers. I asked them how many hours per week a store would have to cut out to have a one percent labor savings, if it had sales of $10,000 per week and paid its employees $4 per hour.

The responses were incredible. One fellow asked me for a calculator. Another said I hadn't given him enough information to solve the problem. Another asked what kind of business it was. None could quickly come up with what seemed to be a very simple answer. One percent of $10,000 is $100. At $4 per hour, to save $100 in a week the company would have to drop 25 hours from the schedule.

But managers shouldn't have to translate, even simple problems like this one. In the heat of competition, communications have to be direct and simple, like when a football team calls audibles at the line of scrimmage.

In that same industry one of our clients came up with a "customers served per person–hour" measurement. It was easy to measure the number of customers per hour and at the same time know how many employees were on duty. At the end of each day the manager figured the customers served per person–hour, and future work schedules were planned accordingly.

The point is that labor control goals are best accomplished by using specific, easily measured quantities. Managers don't have to translate. Audibles cannot be called at the line of scrimmage, as is sometimes necessary, if everyone doesn't have a clear idea of what is going on.

### 7. Goals must contain a deadline.

Remember the 1980 Holiday Bowl between Southern Methodist University and Brigham Young University in San Diego? With three minutes and 57 seconds remaining in the game, SMU was ahead 45–25. The fans were starting to leave, figuring there was no way SMU could lose.

On the following series BYU drove the length of the field and scored on a pass from Jim McMahon (70 NCAA records) to Matt Bragga. BYU failed on a two–point conversion effort, then succeeded in getting the ball back on an onside kick. Several plays later McMahon threw a 40–yard pass to Bill Davis, who went out of bounds on the one–foot line. On the next play BYU scored again and succeeded in the two–point conversion. The score was now 45–39 with less than two minutes to play. This time the onside kick failed and SMU got the ball, forcing BYU to use its last timeout as SMU let the clock run to the maximum on four plays before punting. BYU blocked the punt and got the ball back at midfield with 18 seconds remaining in the game. On the first play McMahon threw the ball away. Eleven seconds remained. On the second play he threw it out of bounds. Three seconds remained.

After taking the next snap, McMahon dropped back further than usual, allowing receivers time to get downfield. Then he threw a perfect, 60–yard strike, right in front of the goal posts. All–America tight end Clay Brown was the intended receiver. Surrounded by SMU defenders he leaped into the air, no time remaining on the clock, and brought down the pass. BYU won the game.

If you don't have a deadline you don't have a goal. Goals must have how much, how many and *by when*.

The most exciting play in all of sports occurs in that last two minutes before the half or the last two minutes before the end of any given period, whether it is a hockey, basketball, or football game.

Deadlines allow the student who has slept in all term, not able to get out of bed before 10 a.m., to stay up all night studying for a midterm exam. Deadlines account for 40% of the money raised in any telethon to be raised during the last 20% of the time. Deadlines are covered in one of Murphy's Laws that says, "The first 10% of a project requires 90% of the time allowed for the entire project to be completed. The second 90% requires 90% of the time allowed for it and that's why it takes twice as long as it should."

Deadlines are the foundation of commitment. Deadlines are the adrenalin boosters. Deadlines are the instigators of achievement and inventiveness. A goals program without deadlines is merely a philosophical statement.

## 8. Goals must contain personality changes.

In 1977 when fullback Todd Christensen was drafted by the Dallas Cowboys, he was told they were going to switch him to tight end. No, he insisted, he was a fullback. Persistent efforts to switch Todd to tight end failed. Finally, he was cut. The New York Giants picked him up, tried him at fullback, then cut him. Finally Todd was picked up by the Raiders, whose offensive philosophy is most similar to Brigham Young University, where Christensen played his college ball. In 1984 Todd Christensen was the leading receiver in the NFL and named to the pro all–star team as a tight end.

You must change too, like starting to get up at 6 a.m., working a full day, cutting out the long lunches.

If you double your income next year, how will you spend it? Where will you put it? Unless you've got some place for it to go, there's no reason to do it or make it. The reason most of us don't make more money than we do right now is because we don't know what we'd do if we had it. You may be laughing at me, but don't.

J. Paul Getty wrote a book called *Being Rich*. Not *Getting Rich*, but *Being Rich*. He talked about responsibilities of wealth and the personality traits necessary to develop and manage wealth. In Paul Meyer's words, "You must first set those goals to *become* before you attempt to set goals to *have*."

The goals to become are the intangible characteristics that make winners what they are. You cannot, for example, become a great skier if you have a strong fear of injury.

If you take an average individual in an average job earning an average income, you can guess that person will probably never get ahead as long as things stay the same. But put that person in a traumatic situation, maybe a costly divorce, a major operation without insurance to cover the costs, any financially taxing situation, and that person will rise to the increased need and generate an increased income. Or he might fall back into the role of a loser and look to someone else, or the government, to meet his obligations. But we can and do change with goals or traumatic experiences. Winners are champions of change and choice.

## 9. Goals must contain an interrelated statement of benefits.

Goals and benefits go together. The acronym WIIFM stands for, "What's in it for me?" Make sure you've got some WIIFM in your goals program.

There is no question that Dorothy Hamill really wanted that gold medal in the 1976 Winter Olympics. Another benefit that most people aren't aware of is that winning a gold medal for an American woman is worth between five and ten million dollars in contracts and endorsements. Dorothy received both. The East German girl who won the figure skating in 1984 has only the gold medal.

When I turn in my sales goals, I translate the bottom line into dollars, break it down into a budget, how much to live on, and what I want to do with the rest.

When preparing your goals, take out a chunk of money just for you after all the living expenses are covered. If it isn't big enough, and you're a salesperson, go back to the sales manager and ask him for permission to raise your goal. Take a paramedic with you.

WIIFM explains the why to people. Anybody, when asked to do something unusual or out of the ordinary, wants to know *why*. They are not as interested in the *how*. Too often we think com-

43

munication is poor when we are trying to shove the *how* down someone's throat when they are still waiting to hear the *why*. But if we can clearly define the *why,* then we will have the kind of performance we want and the *how* will pretty much take care of itself.

Too often we think our communications are not being received or that people are resistant to our requests. This happens most when we are trying to shove something down someone's throat when they still don't understand *why* it's important. The great paradox is that when something didn't get done we go back and ask, *"Why* didn't you do it?"

The *why* in sports is apparent. You wouldn't think of going on a basketball court except to win. You wouldn't think of being in a race unless it was to win or get a better time. You wouldn't think of going hunting unless you hoped to come home with something other than sore feet or a hangover. The *why* is such an integral part of recreation that we sometimes overlook its significance. The *why* also needs to be in personal, business and volunteer activities. Any goal without a benefit statement has no motivational value. Goals must be realistic and obtainable, and they must also carry a promise of reward if achieved.

A good idea in setting goals is to establish an arbitrary reward for yourself when the goal is accomplished. All of us go through life spending money—house payment, groceries, utilities, car payments, clothing. How exciting. When was the last time you told your wife you couldn't wait to finish dinner so you could sit down at the desk and pay the gas bill?

What's so exciting about going out to buy a shirt, a tie, or a suit? But a suit can be exciting if it's a reward for reaching a goal. I'd rather buy a suit as a reward for accomplishing something important to me than because the store puts them on sale. I might pay a little more, but every time I put on that suit the success I enjoyed in reaching a goal will be reinforced. When you have a tangible reward, reaching a goal becomes a *want to* instead of a *have to* experience, and that makes a big difference.

**A record for your record.** If you enjoy albums or tapes, go out and buy yourself a favorite tape or album after reaching a goal. Write on the album cover why you bought it. Buy a record for reaching a record. When you get down in the dumps and can't get yourself going, get out the albums and listen to them. While you're listening, read what you have written on the covers and remember how you got those albums. You won't be down in the dumps after half an hour or half a day of that kind of conditioning. The good get better when they celebrate their victories. And if you have tangible memories of your victories you won't forget them.

## 10. Goals must be realistic and obtainable.

A yard here, a yard there. Woody Hays, one of the great legends in college football, is synonymous with "three yards and a cloud of dust." With that concept Woody dominated Big 10 football for decades. The three–yards–and–a–cloud–of–dust attitude will get you further than any instant accomplishment or get–rich–quick scheme.

If you've never earned very much over $50,000 a year and you've established that as your average for a long time, don't suddenly decide that overnight your earning level will jump to $100,000. Most of us are not capable of making the personality and the work habit changes necessary for such a sudden change in earning ability. But if you set realistic goals and work on them and work on them and work on them, you can get big results. It's like those IRA account advertisements. They say if you start out at age 25 and stick with it you will be a millionaire by the time you retire. Paul Meyer calls that progressive realization. I call it the secret of success. There is a million dollars in your head, if you can just figure out how to get it out. Keep after it.

Generally, reading a self–help book or taking a motivation course invokes little if any change in people. Change is hard to get, frequently like that final yard into the end zone in a championship game. The more realistic and attainable goals are, the greater the chance of seeing some change, at least a little.

Every company must have overall organizational goals, followed by divisional and departmental ones, and then the individual goals of each member of the organization. All must work together.

Sometimes when companies get down to the departmental goals they think that is where goal setting stops. Supervisors are told not to interfere with the private goals of individuals, not to get too close. That's bunk. *Individual goals are the literal foundation of corporate human resource development and planning.*

Individuals are motivated by needs and wants. An organization that not only understands the needs and wants of its workers, but to a certain degree even influences those wants, will be better able to get maximum productivity out of those workers.

Many of us are trained from early childhood not to want. Maybe we learn at church that you cannot be rich and righteous at the same time. We cannot realize our level of motivation until we raise our level of desire, and that means we must be involved in a program of developing wants. When tied to wants and desires, specific goals work.

The clear definition of individual goals is the foundation of teamwork. One time an NBA team lost its all–pro point guard at the beginning of the semi–final playoff series. The other starters changed their play to compensate for the loss of the guard and the team lost the first three games. It wasn't until the coach put in the backup point guard and told the team to play as if the star was in, that the team finally came together and pushed the series to seven games. *Team work is based on great individual execution of assigned responsibilities, not compromise and cooperation.* The minute an offensive tackle looks back to try to cover up for a quarterback who can't take the snap, he is compromising his ef- fectiveness as a tackle and usually winds up on his back watching the quarterback get sacked. Only when everyone excels at his assigned task do we have true teamwork.

On your team, in your business, you cannot achieve great teamwork unless the goals are clearly defined down to the in- dividual level. That is the challenge if you want the motivation of recreation in your business or organization.

# Scorekeeping

*If you can't measure it, you can't manage it.*
*--George Ordiorn*

Have you ever noticed the difference between figure skating and ice hockey crowds? The figure skating crowd offers polite applause when they see a good skating exhibition. On the other hand, the ice hockey fans scream and yell when they see something they like, or don't like, on the ice. What's the difference? Both sports take place on the ice and both involve skilled skaters who have spent many years in preparing to perform.

The reason figure skating crowds are so timid is that they don't know for sure what is happening on the ice. They know someone is skating, but they don't know the score. After the skating is over, the judges flip up their cards--5.7, 5.6, 5.2, 6.0. It is such a bad system that they throw out the high and low scores. And the skater doesn't know if he or she's ahead or behind until it's too late to do anything about it. A terrible scorekeeping system, but until something better comes along, we'll have to live with it.

Ice hockey is different. Every fan and every player knows the score at all times. The team that is ahead knows it and takes appropriate action to protect that lead. The team that's behind knows the score too and can take catch-up action. The fans know the score and can cheer their team to victory.

Scorekeeping is the heart of athletics, and must be the heart of every successful business. What is the first thing news reports mention about any sporting event? The score, who won, the points earned by each team. Then come the stats, the specific measurements of individual and team accomplishments.

In sports, especially professional sports, measurements are continually added to increase interest in the game. Baseball has added what they call the slugging percentage, in addition to the batting average and runs batted in. In golf they have added driving accuracy measurements, putting percentages, number of greens hit and putts per round. Some basketball coaches are monitoring points per possession in an effort to measure the effectiveness of both offensive and defensive strategies.

Every sport has its scorecards, scoreboards, and stat sheets—and so must every business. Business managers must be on constant lookout for new measurements to improve productivity.

The primary responsibility of managers is to set the rules and create the scorecards. Archaic scorekeeping systems, or no systems at all, force employees to wait, wait and wait for feedback from management, thinking "I won't venture beyond where I am until I know how well I did."

Sometimes I am asked how soon scorecards should be set up for new employees. I tell them about Little League baseball. The first day a kid puts on the uniform they start tracking his batting average. They track every hitter and every fielder from the minute he steps onto the field. Yet in business we frequently tell a new employee to sit around for 90 days and then we'll get back to him. Too often all we measure is how the guy combs his hair, what he eats for lunch, or what time he likes to go home. Tracking or scorekeeping must begin on day one.

In ice hockey everybody knows the score at all times. The ice hockey player and his fans aren't worried about pleasing judges. If the puck hits the net, a point is scored. Ice hockey scorekeeping is objective, whereas figure skating scorekeeping is subjective.

In your business, is your scorekeeping more like ice hockey or figure skating? With the availability of the microcomputer, almost every kind of business information is or can be immediately available. Businesses no longer have to wait until the end of the month to know how they are doing. They can know daily, even hourly. Like in ice hockey, businessmen can know the score as the game is being played. Yet, most businesses still have 12 accounting periods just like before World War II. You don't know what you did in March until the middle of April—too late to make any adjustments for March.

There are three ways to manage a company—by observation,

judgment, or measurement.

*Observation management* occurs when John, the sales manager, comes back from a tough sales appointment to find two of his young salesmen sitting on the table in the salesroom laughing and having a generally jolly time. What John doesn't know is that one of them has just written up the biggest contract of the month, and the other has just lined up appointments with the executive officers of two companies John has been chasing for four years.

John doesn't know any of this, and having just been blown out on a sales presentation himself, he's not in a very good mood. As he walks by the salesroom he leans in and says, "Listen, if you guys would get to work we wouldn't be in this sales slump."

Situations like this are occurring in companies all the time.

There are three basic problems with observation management:

(a) It's almost always inaccurate, like trying to judge a book by the cover, or a movie by the preview.

(b) Observation management is not relevant to the process. John observed two guys sitting on a table having a good time. You can't capture all of the events in a single frame. It's like the cheerleader yelling at the referee for making the wrong call while the cheerleader's back was turned.

(c) Observation management is generally negative. There seems to be something in human nature that makes it easier to observe the negative than the positive. Had the two young salesmen been on the phone, John probably wouldn't have noticed or said anything. There's no way to win when you use observation management.

*Management by judgment* occurs when John walks by the salesroom a second time and the two young salesmen are still sitting on the table gabbing. John is likely to make a judgment: "Kids today don't work as hard as I did when I broke into the business."

In some corporations you hear the nautical term, "He can't get rid of his barnacles." That means a guy made a mistake back in 1957 and everybody remembers it. Every time he looks like he's getting close to that same kind of decision they say, "Oh, yeah, you remember when he did that back in..." The danger with management by judgment is that too often generalizations are made from insufficient factual data.

When you have to correct someone, always be ultra–specific. Say "You were 45 minutes late for that Tuesday afternoon appointment," rather than "How come you are always late?" Unfortunately the majority of managers manage by judgment and observation, rather than by measurement. Judgment leads to pre–judgment, which leads to prejudice. Prejudice leads to blindness.

Too often there are negative generalizations—that's when somebody says at 8:30 on a Monday morning that the economy is in tough shape and nobody is buying that day. Too often business people let one or two negative occurrences magnify, mushroom and grow like a cancer, until they make a judgment resulting in a negative generalization. The way to avoid negative generalizations is to be ultra-specific—how much, how many, and by when.

One of the great failures, one of the great culprits in the judgment manager's arsenal is the use of negative generalizations:

"You always did..."

"You never have..."

"You won't..."

*Never make a negative generalization!* Even if you think it is true, it will do more harm than good.

Instead, when describing a negative situation always be ultra-specific. How much are sales down? How many calls did not get made? What specific behavior is it that you are concerned about? Don't make wandering generalities.

*Management by measurement.*

I believe that our progress in business, or life, relates directly to our ability to measure. Four hundred years ago the most portable mechanical timepiece that you could have was a water clock on a wagon. It was 10 feet high, weighed 300 pounds, and you had to pull it around with horses. And it didn't keep good time if the water slopped around. The smallest unit of distance measurement at that time was the distance from King Henry's thumb to his nose, a meter. Everything they built was designed around that unit of measurement.

Today we are much better at measuring things. We have memory chips and integrated circuits. Thousands of numbers can be stored on a surface no larger than a pinhead. Without measuring and counting, such technology would not be possible. Quartz watches are all based on the fact that we can split a second into thousands of beats, the frequency the quartz crystal vibrates. Our progress is based on our ability to improve measurement.

Jim McMahon broke over 70 NCAA records while quarterbacking at BYU. The NCAA has records for almost anything a player can do, and more are added every year to further interest in college athletics.

Comparing business to bowling, the supervisor who believes in management by measurement doesn't hold a blanket in front of the pins while his team members are bowling. He allows each player to know exactly how many pins he knocks down with each ball.

Management by measurement is relevant to the process being measured. The ability to sit on a table and carry on a friendly conversation with another salesman is not relevant to sales success, though too much time on the table can certainly take time away from more productive activities.

*So first, measurement is relevant to the process.* It tells you what happened, especially on the bottom line.

*Second, measurement is usually positive.* By that I mean when you measure something, you get the real numbers. You know where you stand. For example, if I asked you to sit down and create a financial statement, listing all your assets and liabilities, in most cases you'd discover you are better off financially than you thought you were. You are always better off when you know where you stand.

*Third, exact measurements make work as enjoyable as play for the participants because there is a way to win.* When specific measurements are employed, it suddenly becomes possible for the employee to win.

You may be asking, if there are so many obvious benefits to maintaining exact measurements, why then is not more measuring going on? Perhaps some people think it is just too much trouble, maybe too time consuming. Others may be afraid of the truth—suspecting they may not be doing a very good job. They don't think they are winning, so they don't want to keep or know the score. What they don't realize is that they cannot win unless they keep score. There is no way to win without a score.

There are three kinds of workers or players.

*(1) Those who know they are winning.*
*(2) Those who know they are losing.*
*(3) Those who don't know the score.*

It is a fact of life that those who keep score, whether they are winning or losing, win more over the long run. These are the people who accept personal responsibility for their own actions. They would rather know the score while losing than be in the don't know category. The people who achieve financial independence do so by knowing the score. They are the people who set specific goals and keep track of progress towards those goals, even when things are not going smoothly.

I have never met a winner who didn't know the score. I have never met a professional golfer who didn't know who else was on the leader board. People play and modify their behavior based on the feedback of their progress against an acceptable standard—the scorecard.

The great tradition of Notre Dame football is reflected in very subtle fashion on the locker room wall at Notre Dame. As you leave this locker room you can't help but notice all the scores of the great Notre Dame victories over their great rivals emblazoned on those walls. The impact is awesome. Winners keep track of results. Losers keep track of reasons.

George Brett, the great .375–plus hitter for the Kansas City Royals, was asked one time in an interview what his batting average was that day. This was during his quest for the second .400 season.

He said, "I've got 169 hits in 450 at bats. My batting average is .375, and if I go three for four today it will go to .379."

One of the reporters was astonished at Brett's command of mathematics and questioned him on it.

George said, "It's not very unusual. All the .350–plus hitters in the league can tell you what today's performance will mean to their overall batting averages."

But let a reporter ask any of the players batting under .200 what their averages are, and they'll say, "Oh, I'm not sure, a buck and some change," meaning somewhere over .100.

Winners like George Brett understand that there is no joy in victory without running the risk of defeat.

You cannot sit by as a spectator in the game of work. You must in fact trade your season tickets for a pair of shoes and come down on the field, the only place where points can be scored.

Management by measurement is facing the truth, taking away the language and thinking of non–commitment. When you ask someone if he has completed his work goal yet and he says, "basically," "pretty much," or "just about," that means he has accomplished somewhere around 20% of the goal. These verbal diversions are a way to run away from the truth. English teachers call them euphemisms.

Euphemisms, or escape words, exist in business. We terminate or outplace people when, in fact, they needed to be fired. When we haven't finished a job, or even started it, we use words like "basically," "pretty much," or "just about." Avoiding euphemisms vastly improves the level of communications.

There is too much truth in exact measurement for some people. Losers don't have the courage to face the truth of exact measurement. They want to run away from the truth by focusing on activities instead of results. When exact measurements are made, things are brought into clear focus, and there is no place else to hide.

If you have the courage to keep score, even when you are losing, you will win more in the long run. The elimination of uncertainty through scorekeeping increases the ability to take calculated risks.

## The Cash Flow Euphemism

One of the greatest rituals in America today takes place in the private clubs where business leaders meet to eat, exercise and share problems with each other. When I walk into my club, somebody is likely to say,

"How's business?"

You might respond, "Not bad, I just have a little cash flow problem."

The guy that asked the question, and everybody else, would nod their heads knowingly like great patriarchal gods in Egypt and say,

"Boy, we sure know what you mean. We're in the same situation."

What are we saying? How can it not be bad if the cash won't flow, not even dribble a bit?

The mention of cash flow problems is a euphemism, a form of escapism, a way to avoid a very serious business problem. *Cash flow is the barometer of business health.* Saying everything is fine except for cash flow is like saying the patient is fine except for a 105–degree temperature. Businessmen have to pull their heads out of the sand, face their problems and deal with them.

There's no such thing as a cash flow problem. Cash flow problems, as people call them, are really symptoms of deeper problems. Maybe it is not being able to collect the money owed you. It might be that we purchased too much inventory, or the wrong kind of inventory and don't have the courage to liquidate the excess. Maybe we don't have the courage to raise prices and go out and sell value. Or we don't have the backbone to cut unnecessary overhead. I can't cut anybody back even though I have enough help to do 50% more business. Perhaps the owners are bleeding the business by taking more out of the business than it is earning.

On the other hand, if I walked into the athletic club and someone asked, "How's it going, Chuck?" and I said, "Well, not too bad, except I've bought more inventory than I know what to do with. I'm afraid to collect what people owe me. I don't have the courage to raise prices and sell on value. I'm chicken to lay off some of the employees I don't need. I'm bleeding the business by taking out more money than it is earning. But basically, things aren't bad"...if I responded like that, everybody in the club would look at me and say, "Gosh, what a terrible businessman you are. How dare you call yourself a member of this club!"

*There is no such thing as cash flow problems!* This is the biggest euphemism or escape generality in business today. Hitler's propaganda minister Joseph Goebbels said that if a lie is repeated long enough and loud enough everybody will believe it. That's the way it is with cash flow. Smart businessmen look past the cash flow generality to the specific places where their cash flew when they thought it was going to flow.

Cash flow problems do not originate by themselves and cannot be solved as cash flow problems. The roots are deeper. Cash problems originate from five major sources:

*(a) Too much inventory and other non-liquid assets.* Inventory is not being turned over fast enough to justify the cost of holding and handling it.

*(b) Receivables are too high.* Receivables are not being collected fast enough. Perhaps credit policies have remained weak as we have moved into a time of tight cash. Our courage to collect is being dampened by our concern for additional business. Maybe we are operating on the false assumption that sales from people who won't pay are somehow beneficial to our company.

*(c) Inadequate gross profit percentages.* We are unwilling to demand the markup necessary to survive and even prosper when sales are down.

*(d) Unwillingness to implement cost-cutting measures.* I never cease to be amazed at the number of businessmen who think they can increase sales from, say, $5 to $7 million without increasing costs, and if sales drop from $5 to $3 million, they don't think they can decrease costs. When they started their business, sales were at $2 or $3 million with proportionate costs, but they think there is no way they can cut costs back when sales go into a slump.

I acknowledge the fact that some costs are irreversible without doing long-term damage to the organization—space, buildings, real estate—solidly fixed things that have ongoing costs. But it is imperative that we recognize that a building too full of people and inventory can drain off a lot of unnecessary cash. The goal is to find that optimum level of operation where you can achieve maximum profitability and productivity. You've got to be able to bite the bullet.

*(e) Inappropriate compensation for the owner or key decision makers.* An owner or general manager who combines a decrease in profitability with an increase in personal compensation is con-

tributing to his own demise. Farmers don't eat the seed corn. Neither does a good coach.

Too often in business we forget a valuable lesson learned so well on the athletic field--that we don't negotiate the value of points. When a team scores a touchdown on an interception or a fluke play, we don't run over to the field judge and say, "That one is only worth four points." No, the team gets six points, regardless of how easy the touchdown might have been. Yet in business, too often we try to mask the truth with words. We need to get back to firing people instead of outplacing them. We need to return to a communication style that says, "He screwed up," not "His performance is substandard, a little below the absolute minimum required in order to identify and get the job done." We have to have the courage to communicate accurately and have the guts to get to the bottom line.

We have enjoyed the comfortable euphemism of cash flow problems long enough, perhaps too long. If your cash flow has dried up--if it is simply a drip where it used to be a gusher, then look along the pipeline for the holes. Don't be content with the wandering generality that growth, that benevolent dragon, kindly gobbled up your cash and stripped away the profits. Growth is not the good guy unless it is profitable and funded from earnings. Legitimate earnings always were and always will be the best indication of a healthy company.

Remember, there is no such thing as a "cash flow problem" by itself. A shortage of cash is the result of other problems that you can do something about.

Following are some of the basics of good scorekeeping.

*1. Keep it simple.* One time as I was approaching the 18th hole at my country club, a fellow hit a ball that bounced off a rock in a stream, hit a tree, dribbled through a sand trap and rolled onto the green. The resident pro looked over at me and said, "It's a dang good thing the scorecard doesn't make you tell how it happened." A good scorekeeping system just tells how many. A basketball score doesn't tell you about lucky tips or hard-fought rebounds. A football score doesn't tell you how many interceptions were made, or about the dropped receptions that should have been caught, although the individual players who got the tips, blocks, interceptions or fumble recoveries know exactly how many they got, not just for the game but for the entire season, and last year too. Keep it simple.

When an individual keeps his own scorecard, he knows whether he won or lost that day, and also the magnitude of improvement for himself regardless of whether or not the coach had a bad day. The player will also correct any deficiency in his score before the card is turned in. Our self–concept or self–image is based on what we know and can prove about ourselves.

*2. The score is best kept by the player.* A scorecard is most effective when it is kept and updated by the player, as in golf and tennis. That's why three people in a tent can handle all the scorekeeping responsibilities for 140 participants in a PGA tournament, or why four people can handle all the record keeping for a tennis tournament with thousands of participants. Periodically we have clients who make the mistake of having their secretaries do all the graphs and charts, or they make the mistake of having computers print out the scores two or three days after the fact. Self–administered graphing and scorekeeping is the best.

*3. Scorekeeping must offer a comparison between your personal past performance and an accepted standard.* Golf would no longer be a favorite national pastime if the only opportunity for comparison was whether or not you could beat Johnny Miller's record–setting score in the U.S. Open.

Golf survives and thrives because it has a scorekeeping system that allows me to compare myself, an 18 handicapper, with myself. If I go onto the golf course and break 90 I get very excited. I compare my performance to my own past performance as well as to what the pros are doing.

Marathoning has a similar scorekeeping system. How many people would fight and kick and scream to get into the Boston Marathon if the clock was turned off after getting the time for the first place finisher in each category?

The success of a scorekeeping system in recreation depends upon a comparison between your own past personal performance as well as how well you did against the accepted national average. Too often in business we generate a scorekeeping system which only tells how well we did in comparison to an arbitrary, artificially imposed standard.

To sum up the principles discussed in this chapter, consider bowling league competition. Have you ever seen a non–motivated bowler? Everybody knows how to keep score. They throw those balls, jump up and down, and you get the impression they would do almost anything for the prize money.

Work is a lot like bowling, except there's a guy called a supervisor who stands in front of the pins with a curtain. He can see the pins or goal, but the bowler can't. The bowler throws the ball, hears something and says, "How'd I do?"

The supervisor says, "Change your grip."

The bowler says, "But how did I do?"

The supervisor says, "Move your foot." The bowler changes his grip and moves his foot and throws another ball.

He hears the pins fall and asks, "How am I doing?" The supervisor says, "Put some tape in the thumb hole."

"How am I doing?" repeats the persistent bowler.

"Don't worry about it. We've got a review coming up in six months. We'll let you know then."

How long would bowling remain a popular recreational activity under these conditions? Not very long.

**Caution.** The measurement principles discussed in this book need to be introduced carefully into the workplace. There is almost always resistance to change, and the manager or employee who in the past has focused his attention on activity can be intimidated into inactivity by the threat of disclosing performance he may feel is less than acceptable. The truth can be painful and frightening. Employees who are sold on the management by measurement concept and want to get involved of their own free will and choice generally benefit the most from the measurement system.

Too many middle managers today are feeling impotent in their ability to manage, to talk, to create, to discipline, to go, to move, to build with people. Our traditional American management philosophy to manage by exception, to focus on problem areas, to put out fires, results in a reluctance to compliment and praise on a regular basis. We talk about the things that are going wrong, instead of the things that are going right. As a result subordinates are depreciated with more emphasis on shortcomings than accomplishments.

A good scorekeeping system allows the worker or manager to establish his own self-worth in the eyes of his peers, subordinates and supervisors. Everybody becomes more accurately and justly rewarded, stroked, or chastised, based on accurate performance records or scorecards.

# Feedback

*When performance is measured, performance improves. When performance is measured and reported back, the rate of improvement accelerates.*

--Thomas S. Monson

What do you think would happen if Tom Landry approached his team in the locker room before an NFL playoff game and handed quarterback Danny White a piece of paper listing 100 plays in sequence, saying, "These are the plays I want you guys to execute, in the exact order listed on the paper."

Do you think any of the players would object? Of course they would, all of them. They'd think Landry had lost his sanity. Why?

In order for the best possible play to be called in any given situation, it is imperative that the person calling the play have feedback from the last play, or the last several plays--how many yards gained, which lineman is getting eaten up at the line of scrimmage, direction of the wind, which receivers are being left open and which ones are getting double coverage, how many yards remain for a first down or a touchdown, etc.... All this feedback is necessary in order to make the best possible call. Handing a team a predetermined list of plays before the opening kickoff eliminates the use of feedback in calling each play as it is executed. Nobody would be surprised to find out that a team not using feedback would have trouble winning in the NFL, NCAA or even high school.

Yet, how often in business is an employee handed a job description, or a predetermined set of plays, then expected to perform without ongoing feedback? It happens more often than most businesses would like to admit. Feedback is as vital in business as in athletics.

If feedback isn't important, why do we have so many mirrors? Someone once quoted Zsa Zsa Gabor's fourth husband as saying that it wasn't just performance, but comparison to past performances, that made his job so difficult.

When a spouse returns from the beauty parlor––and it could be either sex these days––and says, "How do you like my haircut?" he or she is looking for feedback. The child who has just completed a project in the father's shop or just finished a first attempt at mowing the lawn is always interested in an opinion from a respected peer or superior.

In athletics feedback is more clearly acknowledged and more frequent than in business. When feedback suddenly becomes available in a business situation where it has not been available before, the results can be very dramatic. Let's take a look.

I was called in to consult with a package express company a few years ago. They were concerned, among other things, about the filing of freight bills. They're a federally controlled company and everything has to be filed for possible audits. They file millions of items every year. Their concern was that the four people doing the filing had been three days behind for 36 years, the entire time the company had been in business. The day they opened the door, the filing was three days behind and they had never been able to catch up.

"If you can't measure it, you can't manage it," I said to the supervisor of the people who did the filing.

You can guess her response. "I'm too busy filing them to count them."

One of the vice–presidents with me suggested that the filing could be measured by weighing the stacks of material to be filed. He thought this might work because each piece was the same size and therefore the same weight. Sounded like a good idea to me, but the head filing lady said, "That's the second dumb idea I've heard today."

Finally we told her we were going to try it anyway. We came up with a measurement system similar to the golf handicap. We decided to monitor ounces per person–hour.

"I don't need that stuff," said the head filing lady. "My people work just as hard as anybody else in this company––all the time, every day."

60

"How do you know that?" I asked.

"I've got four file baskets," she said. "Every morning when I get here I spread the filing out equally into four file baskets and hand one to each file clerk, so the baskets are all even."

"What do you do on a heavy day?"

She looked at me like I was a dummy, and said, "Then the baskets are fuller." It was obvious at this point that this lady didn't want to be fooled with, but I persisted, telling her I wanted her to measure by weight the amount of filing going through the department. She didn't want to do it, but she finally agreed to weigh how much each person filed each day.

The first week we came up with an average of 22 ounces per person–hour. We didn't really know if that was good or bad, but it was a start. The next week we developed a scorecard for each worker and taught them how to keep score as if we were teaching them a new game. Each recorded her own ounces per person–hour.

An interesting thing happened. The group average for the second week increased to 33 ounces per person–hour. And by the end of that week they were only one day behind––the first time in 36 years. We were witnessing a miracle.

The head file clerk came to me and said, "Listen, I can't go any faster and be accurate."

"We understand that," I said. "That's all right. Don't worry about it."

The next week production increased to 45 ounces per person–hour. There was no monetary incentive, no threatened disciplinary measures, no promised promotions. The only difference was that we were keeping score, measuring performance. Not only was the department no longer behind, but they were finishing each day's filing by 2 p.m. By the fourth week, production had increased to 54 ounces per person–hour and the filing was finished each day by 11:30 a.m.

I remembered when the head file clerk was doing 18 ounces an hour and telling me she couldn't go any faster. The last time I checked she was up to 72 ounces per hour and trucking. The big payoff was that the four people doing the filing were part of an eight person work force in that department. When two of the non–file clerks quit, for okay reasons, the file clerks came to their supervisor and said,

"Listen, if you'll tell us how to measure what they've been doing, we'll just pick it up."

Like many of you, I receive the Executive Toy mail order

catalogue. They advertise in those flight magazines you find in airplanes and sell all kinds of computerized measuring machines. A recent ad was pushing a $40 pulse meter that goes on the end of your finger while you're jogging. It tells you whether you're living or dying. They've got a $190 radar gun that measures the speed of a baseball in mid–air. The ad says that if you measure your son or daughter's baseball pitch, the kid will learn to throw the ball faster.

The same machine can be mounted on a tripod to measure your tennis serve. These machines are built and sold because the manufacturers and customers understand that when performance is measured and reported back the rate of improvement accelerates.

Probably the most significant achievement in biofeedback involves the heart. If a patient can hear his heartbeat through a speaker system and see the screen on the cardiogram machine, the patient can actually learn to speed up or slow down his own heart. Feedback makes that possible.

Effective feedback is accompanied with its own set of terms, or even its own language, and the most important term in that language is the Results to Resource Ratio––like the ounces per person–hour in the filing example. The successful manager is the person who has the capability of generating a greater result with the same amount of resource. Or the same result with less resource. If he cannot measure it, he simply cannot do it, at least not on a regular, planned basis.

Sometimes we hear about great coaches who have talented players but cannot produce a winning team. They are not able to manage their resources to produce results and they are cut loose.

Every manager, whether he manages many people or just himself, must make a list of all resources available––budget, person–hours, computer time, inventory, supplies, etc. When you get right down to it, a manager is someone who turns resources into results. And the more efficiently he or she can do it, the more successful he or she is as a manager. The Results to Resource Ratio can be used at every level of performance.

You can only chop down a forest one tree at a time. Let the accountants figure the return on investment ratios. This book deals with the micro–measurements, like the ounces per person–hour in the filing example, like Lee Nelson's minutes per bin of bottles described in the foreward. When all the micro–measurements are in place, the macro–measurements will take care of themselves.

I've got a friend named Mooney Player, from South Carolina.

We were doing a session at his company one time when he said,

"Chuck, give me some more pers."

"Excuse me?" I said.

"I said give me some more of them pers, Chuck."

"What are you talking about?" I asked.

"You know," he said, "ounces per person–hour, those kinds of pers."

You might be thinking, "Well that was a great story with the filing company, but what I do cannot be measured like that."

You'd be surprised what can be measured, even on the human side of a business. One time we went into an organization that sold building materials. They'd been on hard times for a few years along with the entire building industry.

They came up with a macro problem, wanting to know what they could do about their labor costs (resource) relative to sales (results).

We told them we had to find a micro–indicator measuring results to resources. We told them it didn't have to have the same scientific accuracy the tax people demand, just something to measure change over a period of time.

First we looked at what they produced. Sales. Dollars. But who knows what's happening to the dollar with its value changing almost daily. We finally determined that we could measure the number of invoices generated by the company. Then we looked at the resource that produces invoices––person–hours.

We went back over the last 18 months of records including 39 pay periods and figured out the number of person–hours per invoice for each pay period. The relationship of human resource to invoice output ranged from as high as 3.7 person–hours per invoice to a low of 1.9 for a two-week pay period. A significant variation.

As we analyzed the ratios, we discovered that the 1.9 ratio occurred when business peaked during the busy summer months. The undesirable ratios occurred during the slow off–season. Earlier, the company had suspected they were labor heavy during the winter months, but they weren't sure how much until we started tracking the person–hours per invoice. With the confidence of exact measurement, management decided they never needed more than 22.5 person–hours per invoice, even during the slack periods.

Now, all this may not sound very sophisticated to the experienced business manager, but that company processed an average of 1600 invoices a pay period. The company was able to cut out almost 2,000 person–hours per pay period. "Who is going to do the work?" you ask. The people that are left, and they are going to do exactly what they have always done. The labor that was removed was expendable, unnecessary, but the company didn't know it until the micro Results to Resource Ratio was developed. In dealing with the human resource, managers must realize that it is flexible and can be managed to do what they want it to do. But it cannot be managed unless it is measured. You can't manage what you can't measure.

Through the years we have found two corollaries that expand on Thomas Monson's original statement that "When performance is measured, performance improves. When performance is measured and reported back, the rate of improvement accelerates."

## Coonradt Feedback Corollaries

**1. Increasing the frequency of feedback improves the quality and quantity of performance.** If you're having a difficult time managing your labor resource and you're measuring it monthly, then go to a weekly measurement. It will improve. If you go to a daily measurement, it will improve again. And if you go to an hourly measurement, it may improve even more.

You may think it will take too much time to administer all these measurements. Meaningful measurement takes no time at all. In the example of the file clerks and in example after example we see that the small amount of time it takes to count results is miniscule when compared with the improved results you are counting.

**2. When feedback is illustrated on charts and graphs the impact is even greater.** In business today we have tremendous amounts of data. It comes in stacks and boxes, making you wonder if the programmers think they are being paid for the pounds of paper they run through the printers. But data by itself is of little value. It must become useful management information, then knowledge that can be used in the decision–making process. Graphs and charts make information easier to understand and digest.

In Chapter 11 we discuss additional examples where specific Results to Resource Ratio measurements resulted in dramatic increases in efficiency and profits.

Remember, in the absence of clearly defined goals and accurate scorekeeping we are forced to concentrate on activity and ultimately become enslaved by it. The goal of every business must be to get to the point where everybody on the team has an individual scorecard. Without clearly defined goals and precise scorekeeping, workers will continue to pay for the privilege of working harder than they work when they are paid.

# Winning

*"Everybody is born with an equal chance to become just as unequal as he or she possibly can."*

--Anon.

Can you list the names of the four teams Pittsburgh beat in the Super Bowl? While you're working on that one, give me the three horses Seattle Slew beat to win the Triple Crown. And then after you get that, give me the five speed skaters that Eric Heiden beat to win his Olympic gold medals.

If you're having a tough time answering these questions, then just tell me who would hit the ground first if the head of the Federal Reserve Bank and the Ayatollah Khomeini jumped off the Empire State Building at the same time. The answer is the same. Who cares? Don't let anybody tell you winning isn't important.

There's a company in Salt Lake City that manufactures NFL insignia merchandise--part of a billion-dollar industry. The biggest customers are 25- to 29-year-old fathers who didn't make it in football and are now hoping that through insignia osmosis the kid will do better.

A huge 42% of all the NFL merchandise sold in 1980 had one of two team logos on it. What were they? The Dallas Cowboys (26%) and the Pittsburgh Steelers (16%). Why? Everybody likes to do business with a winner.

Why didn't they get Mike Krepkie to do the Coke commercials? You don't know Mike? He's a very nice guy. Sat on the bench at Michigan State. He has good posture, his uniform was always fresh and clean. He's better–looking than Joe Greene, the guy Coke picked for the commercials. But Joe is a winner and has the most recognized face in pro football.

Look at it this way. If you accidentally kill somebody with your car, who would you want to represent you in court? The top criminal attorney in the country with over 100 wins under his belt, or some kid still in law school who thinks he can do a pretty good job but has never won a case in court? You would want to go with the winner, of course.

One of the premier high priests of winning in America was Vince Lombardi, former head coach of the Green Bay Packers. He said, "Winning isn't everything, it's the only thing."

The coach was criticized for that statement. Some said he placed too much emphasis on winning, that he should have put more emphasis on sportsmanship. A few years ago some of Lombardi's critics put together a new kind of baseball league for kids in a Texas community. It was like the Little League––the same ball, same bat, same number of innings, same playing field––everything was the same except they didn't keep score. The idea was that there wouldn't be any losers because nobody would know who won.

Do you know how long it lasted? One and a half innings. The kids walked across the street to play sand lot ball where they could keep score. Winning is important!

There's a lot being said today in America about fairness. Everything has to be fair and there are a lot of people who think fair and equal are the same. Winners have a different philosophy that can be summed up in the following: "Everybody's born with the equal chance to become just as unequal as he or she possibly can."

The second thing Coach Lombardi said was, "The objective is to win fairly, squarely, by the rules, but to win." One of his great tackles, a guy by the name of Henry Jordan, has become a phenomenal salesman. Henry was asked one time, "Henry, why do you like to sell?"

He said, "Because of the competition." He explained that every time two people meet a sale is made. Every time a salesman meets a potential customer a sale is made. Either the customer buys the product, or the salesman buys the customer's excuse.

The third thing Lombardi said is, "You don't win once in a while. You don't win occasionally. You don't win by accident. Winning is a habit, just like losing."

Following are eight characteristics of winners.

### One. Winners are prepared.

Winners are ready to play. They don't show up for sales appointments without order forms. They don't show up without a game plan.

George Allen coached the Washington Redskins and took them to the Super Bowl in the mid–'70s. Allen paid a guy for a week to sit on the 30–yard line in the Los Angeles Coliseum, facing west, so he'd know what the angle of the sun would be during the entire ball game. Allen wanted to know which goal to defend when the coin was tossed. Winners are prepared.

How long does it take to reach the Super Bowl? The correct technical answer is 24 hours. That's right, 24 60–minute games—four pre–season contests, 16 regular season games and four playoff contests. Twenty–four hours of playing time to reach the Super Bowl. But how many hours of preparation are involved in preparing for each of those 60–minute games? When you consider the time of the coaches, players, trainers—on and off the practice field—you wouldn't have any trouble counting up thousands of hours of preparation for each of those 60–minute games.

In business, too often our dedication to constant activity eliminates the essential focus on preparation. If we are to be or produce winners in our companies, we must take time to prepare. We must take time to clearly define our Results to Resource ratios for each of our key performers. We must take the time to give them the opportunity to construct a game plan, scout the competition, and build a strategy before we simply send them out to play. Later we'll examine the positive results achieved by an industrial sales company that took time to plan, prepare and establish strategies. Your challenge, Mr. Coach, is to give the same opportunity to each of your players.

### Two. Winners have a positive expectancy to win.

In the 1984 winter games in Sarajevo, Yugoslavia, a young American named Bill Johnson said two weeks before his event that he owned the mountain. He said the downhill was his race, that the course was ready, that he was ready, that nothing was standing between him and the gold. It is typical for winners to talk like this after winning, but not before. Some reporters thought Bill cocky. Some thought him lacking in humility. Some thought his comments inappropriate.

But Bill Johnson saw himself a winner. And on the day when he had to put up or forever shut up, Bill Johnson showed them all. He had programmed his winner computer. He plugged in the software and executed those winning runs, a simple execution of something he already had accomplished in his mind. He had a positive expectancy to win.

Over a decade before, Broadway Joe Namath—upstart, young and cocky—predicted that his team would win Super Bowl III. In the first two Super Bowls the AFL champion had been beaten easily by the Green Bay Packers. And nobody expected the Baltimore Colts to stumble. But Joe Namath had a positive expectancy to win, and he delivered.

Are you, as a player, coach, owner, or general manager, developing those winner attributes in your organization? Are you accentuating the positive, eliminating the negative, and latching onto the affirmative and not messing with Mr. In–Between?

**Three. Winners are specific and positive.** Losers tend to be general and negative. Negativism is the antithesis of a winning attitude. Negativism is the most destructive force that any of us come in contact with, because it robs us of those good feelings we should have about ourselves. Negativism is an evil force. Negativism, if you allow it to penetrate, is like a cancer of the mind.

We had a young man working for us at one time who was assigned the task of setting up sales calls, making appointments. He called in about 4:30 one afternoon, and I said,

"How's it going, Richard?"

And he said, "How do you get past these secretaries?"

"I don't understand," I said.

"None of them will let me see their bosses," he explained.

Anytime I hear a generalization in a negative tone I immediately want to dig into it. I said, "Well, tell me how the day went."

"I made twenty calls," he said. "Fourteen of the bosses weren't even in."

I knew right off that 70% of the secretaries did not refuse to let him talk to their bosses. Their bosses weren't in.

"Tell me about the other six," I said.

"I got two appointments and two guys are going to call me back."

"The other two?"

"One guy had to leave in the middle of the conversation, and the other, well, his secretary...."

See what this salesman did? One of 20 calls went sour, so he made a negative generalization about the whole day's work. When you describe a negative situation, always be ultra–specific. Don't let the wandering negative generality rob you of a positive mental attitude.

Winners see their drinking glasses as half full, not half empty. Winners see the opportunity, losers see the problems. We have heard those comments before. If you have an individual who is constantly looking at the empty half of the glass, you may not want to focus so much on changing his performance as correcting that negative glitch that is hurting his behavior.

### Four. Winners accept personal responsibility for their actions.

Winners say "I," "me," and "our." Losers say "they," "them," "those guys" and "management." There's a language of non–commitment in the world.

We were meeting with the manager of a company one time and I said, "Do you have any problems in this company?"

"Yes," he said. "We have two."

This is going to be easy, I thought. This guy has his problems all netted out.

"What is the first one?" I asked.

"Management doesn't care." As he spoke he extended his right arm straight to the ceiling and locked his elbow.

"What's the second one?" I asked.

"The employees don't care either." He extended his left arm towards the floor and again locked his elbow.

"Can I ask you a question?" I asked. He nodded.

"Which group do you fit into?"

He got this incredible look on his face and said,

"You know, I never thought of it like that before."

He had an acute case of loser's elbow. It's like tennis elbow, that ailment tennis players get when they serve too hard or don't hit the ball dead center. If you shingle a house over a weekend, when you work in an office all week, you get an acute case of roofer's elbow.

Loser's elbow is most common in management and sales meetings. Like when the boss asks why the report isn't finished. Somebody says, "Peggy didn't get it typed." Pop goes the elbow. The boss asks why she didn't get it done. Somebody says IBM didn't get the typewriter cleaned in time. Pop, there it goes again. IBM gets blamed for most of the late reports in the world and "computer" is one of the big words in the vocabulary of non–commitment.

Another big word is "economy." When the boss asks how sales were last month, the elbow goes pop when someone responds,

71

"Well, you know, the economy...."

"Inflation" is another big word in the vocabularies of losers. Inflation is the sum total of all the increases in prices. Generally it affects your revenues as well as your expenses, the net difference being zero. That's all. Yet, the decision–making politicians at the head of our government would like us to believe that inflation is the cause of our economic woes. They've got pains in their elbows, too.

Just as important in the language of non–commitment is "computer." Ever hear of a shipment that didn't get out because of a computer? As if the computer is responsible for pulling the order, walking into the warehouse, and throwing a box on a truck. Incredible. The computer did it! If computers were really responsible for half of what they get blamed for, companies would quit buying them.

Then there is the language of non–commitment related to places. Ever hear a receptionist say with the greatest tone of importance in her voice,

"San Francisco's on the phone."

That would be something, a conference call with eight million people, all at once.

Or the guy who asks about the pay raise he was promised, and is told that Chicago turned him down. And he didn't even know he was on the ballot.

Loser's elbow accompanies the language of non–commitment, the language of losers. Winners say "I," "me," "we." Losers say "they," "them," "those guys," and "the management."

The problem with loser's elbow is that your arm eventually locks in that position, making it tough for you to get through doorways when they open up. Somebody says, "Hey, you did a super job on that project." And you say, "Yeah, but wait until tomorrow...." Winners accept personal responsibility, whether they are winning or losing.

When I'm giving a public speech and want to illustrate the acceptance of responsibility through the language of commitment, I tell the story of Jose and Juanita, a tale that makes a point.

It seems they were going to market early one morning and met at the crossroads.

"Good morning," said Jose.

"I'm not supposed to be talking to you," responded Juanita.

"And why not?" asked Jose, hurt by her blunt reply.

"Jose," she explained. "We are all alone here. There is no one else around. If I were to be friendly to you, you might attempt to steal a kiss."

"Juanita, how could I possibly do that?" he asked, a shocked look on his face, but a slight gleam in his eye. "I am a merchant on the way to market. Underneath one arm I carry a live pig, and in that hand a washtub. Under the other arm I have a melon, and in that hand a live chicken.

"Even if I had a mind to commit such a bold act," he continued, "I could not do so for fear of losing my entire inventory."

"No, Jose," responded Juanita, without hesitation. "You could place the pig on the ground and put the washtub over him. Then put the melon on top to hold it in place. And then I could hold the chicken."

Juanita did not use the language of non-commitment. She was a winner and was willing to take responsibility for her own actions.

Coaches, resolve today to eliminate loser's elbow from your organization. When you are in a sales meeting or a one-on-one conversation and someone starts speaking in the language of non-commitment--"I'm not responsible," "It's somebody else's job"--simply extend your elbow out in any direction, snapping it quickly, and they will begin to understand this all important principle of winning in the *game of work*. We, as coaches, have the responsibility to establish the emotional and attitudinal climate of our team, or our company, or our business--and there should be no place for loser's elbow, the language of non-commitment.

**Five. Winners don't seek to change the rules.** They seek only to understand them well enough to win.

In 1980 the Los Angeles Lakers played the Philadelphia '76ers for the NBA title. Game five was in Los Angeles. Suddenly Kareem Abdul-Jabbar tore a muscle in his leg. Not only was he out for the game, but for the series. The man, and the franchise, couldn't make the trip for game six in Philadelphia.

Now, the moment Kareem got hurt, the Los Angeles coach jumped right up and marched over to Billy Cunningham, the '76er coach and said,

"OK, Billy, the big guy's hurt. Which two big fellows are you going to keep on the bench? Got to keep this thing fair."

You don't remember that? Maybe they cut away for a commercial.

Of course you didn't see it. That's not the way winners behave.

The Los Angeles Lakers got on the plane and went back to Philadelphia, not complaining about the loss of their star. They took a rookie, a kid who couldn't vote in a lot of states because he was only 20. He was 6'8", and they put him in the middle against Daryll Dockins, the man they call Chocolate Thunder because he smashes glass backboards for sport.

In the sixth game against Philadelphia, the 20–year–old rookie scored 42 points, pulled in 18 rebounds, and dished out 11 assists to lead Los Angeles to the NBA title. His name is Magic Johnson. He went to Michigan State. His team demolished Larry Bird's team on their way to the NCAA championship in 1979. Magic learned early that the rules don't change, that it's your performance that you are judged on.

Winners don't try to change the rules. They only seek to understand them well enough to win. Think about all the people that are trying to change the rules today. They are trying so hard to make things fair and equal that they never get into the real game and go for the win.

We will always have leaders and followers, winners and losers, people who add to and people who take away. A lot of things need changing, but winners don't try to change the rules in the middle of the game, they only seek to understand them well enough to win.

Jay Van Andel, one of the founding partners of the Amway Corporation, delivered during his service as chairman of the board of the United States Chamber of Commerce a speech containing a truly great quote about a lesson this country needs to learn: "We are not going to help the caboose catch up to the engine by stopping the train." Certainly we need to seek change and improvement, but too many people are trying to change the rules for an easy shortcut or a free lunch so they can get the benefits of winning without having to play the game.

### Six. Winners pay the price--willingly because they know it's a bargain.

How many times have you heard this one?

"If you want to be a winner, Carol, you've got to pay the price."

And they always say it like they just had a dill pickle.

"Pay the price, it's going to hurt."

"No pain, no gain."

"Take another ten laps. Don't stop when the blisters pop."

Losers pay a price too, but winners pay it *willingly*.

Eric Heiden is a real winner. He won five gold medals at Lake Placid. Best individual performance ever in the Winter Olympic Games. He is from Wisconsin. His schedule included starting on the university soccer team and then running the 289 steps up the ski jump hill. Plus, he skated in those sub–zero winters wearing that skinny racing suit.

But he didn't train outside all the time. He has a training room equipped with a stainless steel platform about 7 1/2 feet wide with a four–inch lip around the edge. In training for the Olympics he got on the platform and exercised four hours at a time, day after day, week after week, year after year. They showed it on television, and what kind of expression do you think was on Eric's face?

There was no agony, pain or disappointment. Just a smile, the expression of a winner. And behind the camera, in full view, Eric could see a picture of the gold medals he was going to win. Winners pay the price willingly because they know it's a bargain. And when you concentrate on the end result, the obstacles melt away in the intensity of the preparation.

Winners are more willing to pay the price as the coach becomes more skilled at painting vivid pictures of the end results or benefits. Putting the *why* into our communication brings about incredible performances from the players.

### Seven. Winners are goal setters.

Winning and goal setting are synonymous. You can't win unless you know what victory represents. You have to know when to take the cork out of the bottle. There are a lot of people who work just as hard as the people who win––they just never figure out when to stop and celebrate. But most of all, winners are goal setters.

Let me take you back to 1959, San Francisco, Keezar Stadium. This story has been told at a lot of banquets and written up in a number of publications. From what I have heard and read, this is the way it happened.

In Keezar Stadium there's a football game going on, the San Francisco '49ers against the Cleveland Browns. On the field for Cleveland, from Syracuse University, All American, All–Pro Mr. Football of the late '50s, is running back #32 Jimmy Brown. Jimmy had a good season up to this point and is chewing up all the NFL rushing records.

While Jimmy is picking up yards on the playing field, there is the usual flock of kids hanging around outside the gates. One of them wants to get in. He wants to meet Brown. He's having a little trouble because he doesn't have enough money for a ticket. He's got another problem too. He's from the North Beach ghettos, and due to a neglected diet he has rickets––a disease practically unknown in the 20th Century. His legs are bowed as a result of the disease. He is wearing steel splints to walk. He is ten years old.

The boy waits until the third quarter when the guards finally leave the gate. He sneaks into the tunnel and stations himself there (like the kid in the Coke commercial with Joe Greene), and he waits for the end of the game.

When the game is over Brown comes off the field—muddied, bloodied and battered. He walks toward the showers. The boy steps out in front of him and says, "Mr. Brown, can I have your autograph?"

And Jim Brown, as he must have done thousands of times in his career, takes the pad and pen, scribbles his name, hands the stuff back to the boy, and continues his journey to the shower.

The kid isn't through with him, so he reaches up and tugs on the jersey. Jimmy Brown turns around. The kid brings himself up as tall as he can in his steel braces, looks Brown in the eye, and says, "Mr. Brown, I want you to know I have your poster in my room. I watch you on television every chance I get. I know about all the records you hold, and I think you're the greatest runner in football."

Brown, caught up in the boy's intensity, says, "Thank you, son. I appreciate that." And he turns again to the shower.

But the boy isn't finished. He tugs on the jersey again, brings himself to his full height for a second time, and says, "Mr. Brown, I want you to know one other thing. I'm going to break every record you hold."

Brown holds the boy's stare and says, "What's your name, boy?"

And the young man says, "Simpson, sir. Orenthal James Simpson."

This is a true story. Jimmy Brown and O.J. tell it almost as much as I do. O.J. went on to win the Heisman Trophy at USC. He played for Buffalo and San Francisco in the NFL and broke all but three of Jimmy Brown's records.

Winners are goal setters, and the rise or fall of every organization is based on the ability of individuals in those organizations to set and achieve goals. Setting a clear goal will give you more motivation than someone holding a gun to your head or a thousand dollar bill in front of your nose.

Remember Dorothy Hamill? She won a gold medal and the world figure skating championships at age 17. Then she landed a lucrative advertising contract with Clairol.

Dorothy set her goal when she was six years old. She got up at 5:00 in the morning and practiced for two hours before school, where she maintained a B–plus average. After school she practiced for two more hours, day after day, week after week, year after year—for eleven years until she reached her goal. Goal setting is the strongest force in the world for human motivation.

But you don't have to be an Olympic athlete or a professional football player to make this stuff work. You don't have to start as a kid, either.

In his autobiography, Harlan Sanders tells about the Great Depression. He said he thoughtfully planned a scheme for kidnapping and holding for ransom the child of a wealthy neighbor to buy food. He was flat broke four times. He was cooking chicken in his wife's restaurant because he couldn't make it in the motel business.

The Colonel cooked his first piece of Kentucky Fried Chicken at 39 South State Street in Salt Lake City when he was 65 years old. When he came back a few weeks later the place had gone wild. Everybody wanted that Kentucky fried chicken.

At 72 he sold out to Johnny Y. Brown (Mr. Phyllis George for those of you who know football, and also the former governor of Kentucky). The Colonel received $2 million plus $250,000 a year in personal appearance contracts.

Harlan Sanders has the most recognized face in the world, next to Mickey Mouse. At age 88 he was asked if he had any more goals.

"Yup," he said. "I've got three of them. Number one, I'd like to live 12 more years and become a centenarian. Second, at 100 I would like to take two years off because I haven't had a vacation since I cooked that first piece of chicken and I'm gettin' tired. Third, after I get off my vacation at 102, I'd like to come back with a new idea and make another major impact on American life." Leukemia took him at age 90, so he never reached those last goals. Still, goal setting is the strongest force in the world for human motivation.

Three percent of the people in the United States are financially independent. Do you have any idea what the net worth might be for the people at the bottom of that select category? A million dollars, perhaps?

Not quite. According to the 1982 report of the Research Corporation of America, less than one–half of one percent of the people have a net worth of over a million dollars. Three percent of the people have a net worth exceeding $300,000.

Ten percent of the people have net worths between $150,000 and $300,000. They earn between $40,000 and $60,000 a year. These people are comfortable, or at least they are reported to be.

Sixty percent of the people in the United States barely make a living. Their net worth is tied up primarily in the homes they live in, and is mostly offset with charge card balances.

Twenty-seven percent of the people need some form of support just to survive on a daily basis. It fluctuates depending on who's in the White House.

What do you think distinguishes the top two groups from the bottom two, other than the fact that the top two are where everyone wants to be? As Sophie Tucker said, "I've been rich, and I've been poor. I believe rich is better."

The top two groups are goal-oriented, while those in the bottom group have few goals, if any. Still, the 3% group, on the average, outperforms the 10% group 50 to one. The average net worth of the 3% group is many times greater than the average net worth of the 10% group. Yet there are no demographic differences between the two groups—no significant differences in age, race, religion, education, sex and parental wealth.

The big difference is that the people in the 3% group have written goals with specific plans for reaching those goals. Not very many people are willing to do that.

Why don't people like to set goals? Why don't people like to write them down? Some people don't like to measure performance. Fear of failure, perhaps. Some people are lazy. But look what they are passing up. Rich people live longer, better and seem to be more happy. And contrary to all the publicity, the people in this group have fewer divorces.

Franklin D. Roosevelt constructed his plan for the presidency of the United States 20 years before he was elected. The world's greatest and most beautiful buildings, bridges and airplanes are first created, in elaborate detail, on the drawing board before the first brick or piece of metal is set in place. Written goal setting allows one to transfer the dreams of his mind into a specific plan that can be handed to others to work on. Written goal setting is not an opinion or a whim or a wish floating about in someone's dreams. Written goal setting is the key step that turns dreams into reality.

Coaches, create your own written plan. Be an example to your players. Share with them the power that comes from the creation of a written plan for prosperity. Become the architect of your own accomplishments.

### The Challenge

I will end this chapter on winning by telling you about Fred. He was a college football player from the Midwest. He came out of a small school in Indiana. Fred wanted to be a professional football player. He played well in college and was drafted by the pros.

Fred was about 5'10", weighing about 220 pounds. He was an

offensive guard. He went to camp, studied the play book, and did everything everybody else was doing. He really worked hard.

He got cut and went back to Indiana. They said, "Fred, why don't you coach? We have a good high school opportunity. Why don't you coach?"

"Nope," said Fred. "My goal is to be a professional football player." So he went and worked out on the weights and read the play books, and went on a see–food diet (every time you see food you eat it). He bulked up and got bigger and stronger. He put on 15 pounds and went back to try again.

They gave him a second chance. He worked out. He paid attention. He was enthusiastic. He had a positive mental attitude. He did everything a winner should do. He got cut again, the second year in a row. He went home.

Again they said, "Fred, why don't you go coach?"

"I don't want to coach," he said. "I want to be a professional football player."

Again the diet. Again the weight training. Another year dedicated to that kind of thing. He worked in a steel mill, and at other odd jobs to support himself.

The third year he was back at training camp again. Bigger, stronger, better at everything a football player should do. And he knew the plays.

He got to the final cut this time. Almost made it.

He went home, thinking maybe they were right. Maybe he should coach.

But after thinking about it, he thought, "No, I want to be a professional football player."

He obtained his free agent status and the next season signed up with the worst team in the league, the Green Bay Packers, who had had a one and eleven record the previous season.

Fortunately for Fred, the head coach was another short, fat, dumpy guard from Fordham University. This time Fred "Fuzzy" Thurston didn't get cut, and nine months later he suited up for the NFL Pro Bowl.

Rejected three times, encouraged by the people who loved him most to give it up, Fred Thurston demonstrated the last quality of a winner. Winners don't quit. I remember being told you cannot fail until after you decide to quit. Winners never do.

# Attitudes of Winners

*If you are going to be a successful duck hunter you must go where the ducks are.*

                                        --Chuck Coonradt

## Winners are specific

In 1978, when I was just beginning to see the many parallels between sports and business and was seeking answers about the winning philosophy, I decided to interview some real winners. I got on the phone and called Alabama. I wanted to talk to Paul "Bear" Bryant, who has since passed away but was then head football coach at the University of Alabama.

I just dialed the area code and asked for "The Bear." Immediately, the operator put me through to the man who became a legend in his own time. In 1982 the Alabama legislature met to pass an exception to its mandatory retirement law at age 70. The addendum stated that the Bear could work for the state of Alabama as long as he pleased. That's how much they think of that man in Alabama.

When I got him on the phone I asked him if he was a winner. He growled back at me and said,

"I won 307 football games. I won 88.7% of all the ball games I ever coached."

I got the message. He was specific. I thanked him for his time and hung up the phone.

Then I called the head football coach at a local state university, a major university with national recognition in many areas, thinking he too would know about winning. I got him on the phone and asked the same question, if he was a winner.

He said, "Chuck, you've got to understand something."

Right away I knew I was in trouble.

"You've got to understand," he said, "that I've got the seventh smallest budget in the conference. If I finish higher than seventh, I'm not doing bad."

I thought maybe he didn't hear me, so I repeated the question. "Coach, are you a winner?"

"Chuck," he said, "you've got to understand that they don't support football in this town the way they do down the highway (at the conference champion school.)"

I thought I'd give him one more shot. I said, "Coach, are you a winner?"

He said, "Do you know how hard it is to get those kids from Southern California to come up here and play football?"

The coach reminded me of a retail clothing store I did some work with. We were just getting started. I was interviewing the president of the company and asked him what he would like most for us to do for him.

"I'd like to have you stop the weather reports," he said.

I didn't know what he was talking about and asked him to explain. He did.

"I've got these eight retail stores out there," he began, "and every time I call up and ask how sales are they give me the weather report. If I ask if everybody showed up for work, they say it's snowing and the people couldn't get in. Or the customers had to stay home because it's raining. Just stop the weather reports!"

What this manager really wanted was for us to get his employees looking at the scorecards and goals instead of making excuses for bad performance.

## Winners play the odds

One time a bleeding heart reporter was interviewing Willie Sutton, famous bank robber. The reporter was trying to gain insights into the criminal mind in an effort to better understand criminal behavior.

"Willie, why do you rob banks?" asked the reporter in all sincerity.

"Because that's where the money is," responded Willie.

Winners understand probabilities. They go where the money is. They understand the Pareto Principle. Pareto, history tells us, was a little Italian sociologist who studied tax rolls and tax rates in Italy and concluded that 20% of the property owners paid 80% of the property taxes. I don't know what that discovery did for Mr.

Pareto, but I know it is a hot subject in business circles. You and I know it as the 80–20 Principle.

I had the opportunity to work with a communications firm one time that was leading in its market. They had it made. I remember one of their salesmen, a seven–year veteran, a man well past the middle of his life. He was the kind of individual who's typically hard to motivate because he already has most of the material things he wants in life. He was the number four producer in the sales network, one of those solid individuals you just build the company around. He was the good old boy.

As we began to meet, he was always saying that he was too busy for our goal–setting gimmicks. He had a lot of work to do, things that had to be attended to, and people to call on—hustle, hustle, hustle. Our goal setting wouldn't work for him because we didn't understand his business and we didn't understand the market.

He was a hustler, a hard worker. He had a plan. He would go out and work hard, hope he sold a lot, try to develop new accounts, get that extra business, make the goals, and he knew he was really good. The commission checks just rolled in. He was typical, too typical.

We introduced him to the 80–20 Principle—that 20% of his accounts produced 80% of his business.

"Chuck," he responded, "you just don't understand this business very well at all."

As we continued our debate I asked him to consider the investment in our services his company had already made, and asked him to try it my way, just once. I asked him to take his previous year's sales records and go back and calculate how much of his business came from each customer and to rank them according to dollars spent with him.

He reluctantly agreed to follow my suggestion and returned just a week later with a satisfied look on his face, as if he had proven something to somebody.

"You said that 20% of my accounts would be 80% of my volume," he said.

"That's true," I responded.

"You were wrong," he said. But along with that look of satisfied defiance, I noticed a little hint that he may have learned something as well.

"How far off was I?" I asked.

"The top 19 accounts, out of a total of 104, accounted for 83% of my business," he said, as he and the rest of the people in the room began to laugh.

"I want you to know too," he continued, "that another six of my accounts produce the next 13% of my volume, and that 25 of my 104 accounts produced 96% of all the dollar volume I did last year."

"How do you feel?" I said.

"Wonderfully embarrassed."

"What are you going to do now?"

"I'm going to take the bottom 40 accounts," he said, "and lay them on the sales manager's desk with a note that I don't deserve to work with them."

He did that, and the sales manager was shocked and immediately created a draft pool to redistribute accounts to new salespeople.

The salesman said he was going to major on the majors. He laid out a schedule over the next 90 days to meet with each of his accounts in descending order from the largest to the smallest. The time that would have been spent on the 40 accounts he didn't have anymore was used to identify and penetrate into new business that had potential to compete in size with his best clients.

Four months later he told me he had just received his largest commission check since coming to work for the company. He had paid off a couple of second mortgages on his different investment properties, and he and his wife were enjoying a lifestyle unparalleled in their history. An understanding of the 80–20 Principle had enabled him to major on the majors, thanks to a simple scorekeeping technique.

Incidentally, he came into our program with a 13% sales increase goal. Ninety days later he revised it to 47%, then exceeded that and achieved a 55% increase in sales the first 12 months after utilizing a tracking system that enabled him to major on the majors. The tracking system enabled him to motivate himself without outside pressure, to realize more of his own untapped potential.

The 80–20 Principle can be graphically illustrated for any business or sales person as shown on the chart on the following page.

# Annual Dollar Volume From Customers

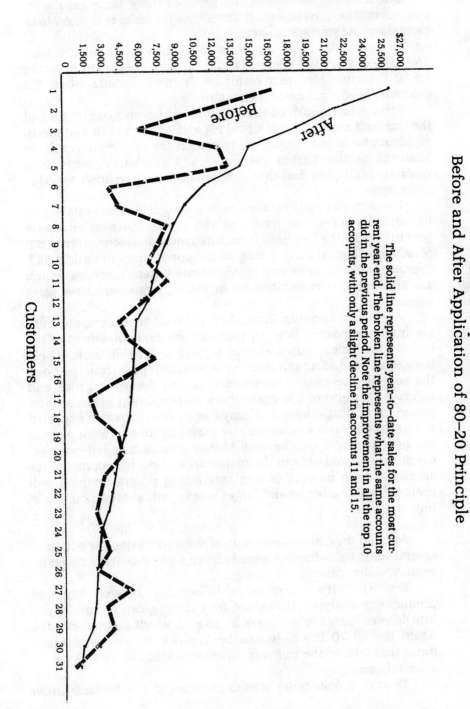

## Client Expenditures
### Before and After Application of 80-20 Principle

The solid line represents year-to-date sales for the most current year end. The broken line represents what the same accounts did in the previous period. Note the improvement in all the top 10 accounts, with only a slight decline in accounts 11 and 15.

Majoring on the majors can produce these same results for your team. The marketplace defines how the team is doing. Major on making the strong stronger.

In industrial sales accounts there is a fairly safe, yet aggressive—if you can believe that combination—application of the 80-20 Principle that can result in dramatic results when the customer base is reasonably constant.

First, take the 20% of the accounts which account for 80% of the business and establish a goal for a 25% increase in that group of accounts. If accomplished, this increase can replace all the business obtained from the other 80% of the accounts. Any business at all from the other 80% will be increased business. This is the first step.

The second step is to take the next 40% of the accounts which traditionally accounted for about 16% of the business and set a goal to double the business from this group of accounts. This is a reasonable, logical plan, giving us the opportunity to build a 32% increase into our sales and still generate excess accounts which are available for redistribution to young, aggressive new sales people.

Western Leadership Group has had a lot of success, and fun, teaching companies how to manage the pool of left-over accounts. We have set up a system similar to the NFL draft, where the lowest producing salesman gets first draft pick from the pool, the next-to-the-lowest salesperson getting the second pick and so on. At the end of the draft, the salespeople are given a short period for trading. Then, in 30 days, each salesperson is expected to turn into the sales manager a written plan of attack for each of the new accounts. At the end of this process any left-over accounts are turned over to the inside order desk to become house accounts, or to be part of a telemarketing program which will eventually play a larger and larger role in industrial account selling.

Another dramatic application of the 80-20 Principle occurred several years ago when we were helping a paint distributor get inventory under control.

Frequently it's necessary to differentiate between types of productivity analyzed. Inventory, for example, can be subdivided into different items or groups of items with varying turnover rates. Again the 80-20 Principle can be applied. We've heard many times that 20% of the items in inventory account for 80% of the sales volume.

The paint distributor was committed to the no back order

philosophy. The president insisted that all of the items asked for by customers would be in present inventory. We asked him how he measured it, how he tracked individual products. He said he didn't need to because he had established a company goal to have everything in stock 100% of the time, a goal so often emphasized that it simply didn't need to be tracked.

Finally, after much discussion, he agreed to spend $10 worth of a clerk's time to measure the company's actual ability to have on hand the desired product 100% of the time. We discovered during the first week, in the middle of the prime selling season, that 17% of the orders couldn't be shipped because of insufficient inventory. The president was flabbergasted.

"We can't have this," he said. "It must have been an unusual week."

We agreed to continue the tracking, and in the second week 16% of the orders couldn't be shipped because of insufficient inventory. The president was beginning to listen. He agreed to let us continue the scorecarding and tracking until we achieved the desired results.

Within two and a half months we had the number of unfillable orders down to 6%. But we weren't satisfied. The inventory was too large. And there was some question about the value of our measurements.

We acknowledged the 80–20 Principle, agreed that there needed to be differentiation between different inventory items, but more emphasis where the greater problems existed. We divided the inventory into three groups. Exactly 20% of the items fell into Group A, which comprised 78% of total sales. Management resolved to never be out of stock on these items. We tracked them separately from the other two groups.

The middle group (B) consisted of 40% of the items responsible for 17% of sales. We all agreed these were necessary items to stock, but not imperative for the success of the organization. Frequently these items were the same product as in Group A, but in different sized containers. Sometimes they were paints where the color was just a shade off the Group A color. Often substitutions could be made if these items were out of stock. We determined that with Group B items the company could maintain a higher risk of running out.

Group C items, the bottom 40% of the inventory items, accounted for less than 5% of total sales. The president was amazed that he had so much money tied up in such a small part of his business. It was obvious that the company could accept a much higher out–of–stock risk with items that made up such a small part of the business. We concluded that with many of the items it would be better to air freight them in than tie up so much capital in inventory.

We established criteria for each inventory level, measured by weeks on hand. In Group A we decided that in the peak season we would attempt to carry an eight–week supply. In Group B we decided to carry a two–week supply, maintaining a six–week average for all inventory. For Group C (5% of the business) we maintained no safety level, just one item on the shelf to be reordered when it was sold.

We began to beef up orders for Group A items to get to the eight–week level, and we reduced orders for Group B and Group C items. As we finished the busy season we had reduced the inventory from $290,000 to $165,000 and banked $115,000 of former operating capital, while maintaining a customer order satisfied record of 93%. By keeping score you can have your cake and eat it too.

In business we often hear—and my father the grocer has repeated it many times—that we cannot afford to ignore any customer. Every one is important. There is a measure of truth in these statements. Still, applications of the 80–20 Principle occur so often and with such force that it cannot be ignored.

If you are going to hunt ducks you must go where the ducks are. And if you are going to kill giants, you must spend your time in the beanstalks, not in the pea vines. After consulting in detail with hundreds of businesses, I don't hesitate to say there are applications of the 80–20 Principle in every business.

Remember, winners expect to win. With the 80–20 Principle applied to sales customers or inventory behavior, your research will develop within you a desire as well as an expectation to win.

# Field of Play

*Don't change the rules in the middle of the game.*
--Chuck Coonradt

Do you remember Rosie Ruiz in the Boston Marathon a few years back? She finished first among the female contestants. Her time, compared to her past performances, was unbelievable. Then we found out she hopped on a bus, outside the Field of Play, outside the rules of competition. She had finished the race, but her performance was not within the criteria established by those who controlled the race. Her time was not recorded in the record book, and they do not have a Boston Marathon bus ride trophy. The Boston Marathon has a clearly defined Field of Play, and Rosie got herself into trouble trying to perform outside the Field of Play.

In organizations of every kind we hear the cry to improve communication, or to eliminate the communication problem. Improving communication is the topic of millions of conversations every day. This problem isn't nearly as serious on the playing field among athletes. How many of the 60 or so plays in a football game are not communicated to the players? Very few, if any.

In an effort to solve the communication problems, we've seen the era of transactional analysis with the upfront contracts. We've had the job description writers and I must admit an incredible bias against their efforts--mainly because of the lack of specificity and the necessity of the Supreme Court to interpret the language of many job descriptions. A client of ours, a president of a company generating net profits in the millions, had a 14-page job description and the only numbers contained therein were the page numbers at the bottom of each page. It's very difficult to understand success and failure, winning and losing, good and bad, in that morass of confusion.

We have gone through sensitivity training and empathy building and role playing, but to understand the principles in this book, we need only to look at our great athletic and recreational past.

Prior to or synonymous with the development of goals certain criteria must be established in reference to the Field of Play. In fact, the Field of Play is defined well in advance of the placement of goals.

When Dr. Naismith hung that first peach basket up on the barn wall and started the game of basketball, he had to define the dimensions of the Field of Play. He had to identify to the players when their baskets would count and when they would not, where they could dribble and where they would be out of bounds. And when Abner Doubleday organized the sport of baseball, the primary improvement he brought to the previous activities of throwing rocks at squirrels and hitting chestnuts with sticks was the design and dimension of the Field of Play with boundaries and rules.

If you were given several acres of raw ground and given the assignment to lay it out for maximum utilization for a sports center, one of the design techniques would be to take scale models of the various fields of play and begin arranging them on that plot of ground in order to get maximum or optimum utilization of space. It would not make sense to stick a basketball standard here and a hockey goal there and a soccer goal over there and a baseball backstop over here without knowing the ramifications.

You can't go out and start playing until the Field of Play is clearly and completely established. The boundaries, or the Field of Play, must be in place before you can set the goals and begin to play the game. Even in a casual game of touch football or sand lot baseball, the kids will decide the boundaries before they start playing.

In athletics the Field of Play is so indigenous as to be almost taken for granted. If I say, "Let's go play tennis," you correctly assume that we're going to a tennis court. If I say, "Grab your golf clubs," your only question is which course are we going to play on.

The shape of the field says so much about the nature of the game that it is incredible to me that we have not done a better job in American business in defining the Field of Play before we just run off with a station wagon loaded with equipment, or drop a new personal computer on a manager's desk.

Our problem, I think, lies in the fact that in recreation the fields of play exist already. They've just always been there. So we walk onto them and accept the assumptions they give us without really thinking about them. We've never had to create fields of play, and we have not been taught how to do it. Let's look at some options.

What shape is a Field of Play in basketball? A rectangle. What shape is a tennis court? Again rectangle. A football field is a rectangle too. What shape is a race track? Oval. A baseball diamond is not a diamond, but actually a square, and if you look at the entire field you find a quarter of a round. We couldn't play any of these games without first accepting the standard Field of Play.

What do you think would be the reaction at the New York City Athletic Club if an unknown college running back walked in the door and announced that he had come for the Heisman Trophy?

"But I rushed for over 3,000 yards this year!" claims the player as he is led to the exit.

"We don't have any record of that."

"Ask the coach. He saw me. I did it during practice."

"But that doesn't count...."

The point here is that if you are going to play a game you've got to know where the out-of-bounds markers are. You must have a general overview of the field of competition. You can't play golf without greens, fairways and tees; you can't play golf without a Field of Play.

You may be wondering why I even bother to discuss such an obvious principle. I do so because you can find hundreds of business examples--common, everyday occurrences--where people are expected to perform without knowing the Field of Play. Our ability to overlook the obvious is incredible.

Consider the employee who has just come out of a retail store staff meeting where he has been chewed out for allowing excessive customer returns.

"We took back a $35 gadget yesterday that was purchased almost a year ago," scolded the manager. "How can we expect to make money when employees are that ignorant of company policy?"

Two hours later the employee is unknowingly waiting on a good friend of the manager who wants to return something that wasn't purchased in the store. The manager knows she is a very good customer. The employee knows what he heard in the morning meeting. The manager and the employee have different perceptions of the Field of Play, which has never been clearly defined.

As the employee courteously explains to the customer why the company cannot accept the returned merchandise, the manager walks up and says,

"Good morning, Mrs. Fishburg. How are you? Glad to have you in our store today. Of course we'll take your return."

The employee, who was trying to do the right thing, is suddenly confused, maybe even embarrassed. Uncertainty is very high. The Field of Play is no longer clear. A painful personal memory has been created, and for the rest of the day that employee would just as soon hide in a corner.

Can you remember a situation in your business where someone overstepped their bounds, played outside their sandbox, messed up someone else's job because they didn't have a clear understanding of their Field of Play? You can probably think of lots of examples.

Can you think of anyone in business with a clearly defined Field of Play? Someone who works in an environment of absolute certainty with clear policies and procedures? Clear work rules, security, guarantees, a certain amount of vacation, a person who knows exactly what to do every day? You might have in mind someone who works on an assembly line or perhaps runs a mail sorting machine at the post office. You may think people with such jobs are not happy because they are not challenged. They don't have the variety, fun and risk that you have, but they do have a high comfort level, a very high degree of certainty.

Freedom is greatest when boundaries are clearly defined. When I know exactly where the edge is I am more confident. I would rather be following a police officer in his car than be concerned about him hiding with his radar gun. I would rather drive on a treacherous patch of icy road when I have clear vision than I would when I'm in the fog. My freedom and security are greatest when my boundaries are clearly defined.

I was driving with a broken speedometer cable to a city 30 miles north of my home one day. I was late for an appointment and I'd received two speeding tickets in the previous 90 days. One more and they would take away my driver's license. The uncertainty was incredible.

I'd look at my watch and be reminded that I was running late. I would speed up. Then, realizing I was passing other cars, I figured I was going too fast and would slow down. Every time I came over a hill, I fully expected to see a highway patrol car with a radar gun waiting for me. Gradually the uncertainty forced me to restrict my performance, to shrink back. Since I didn't know where the boundaries were, I had to restrict my performance in an effort to avoid going out of bounds. With two speeding tickets already, I simply couldn't take that risk. Had my speedometer been working, I could have moved comfortably to the very edge of the boundary at 55 miles per hour without any anxiety, knowing I was within the Field of Play.

Sometimes we find ourselves in a Field of Play shaped like a donut. We have a large area of responsibility and a small area of authority. This is the frustration of many people in administrative roles or staff positions who are given broad parameters of what line management expects, but little authority to carry out those expectations. Their response is to wander about the company saying, "Charlie told me...," "Charlie says...," "Charlie wants us to...," and they are never really sure about the authority they represent and can find no satisfaction in their own authority. The donut, unfortunately, beomes a center where very little is accomplished.

In the early '80s there was a mad rush into the home computer field, with dozens of companies competing vigorously for market share. Rebates and price cutting were the common fare as manufacturers pushed their wares on confused retailers. The result was an oversupply of home computers, resulting in downward price pressure. Two and a half years into the decade, most of these aggressive computer manufacturers not only found themselves without profit, but in a struggle for survival. No one bothered to set the boundaries before they started to play the game. Market sizes, demographics, buying patterns and customer profiles were not clearly defined. Without a clear Field of Play, the result was chaos.

A common Field of Play in business is shaped like an amoeba—a random, globular shape. It describes the employee's understanding of what he thinks is expected of him, and the only problem is that it wiggles and jitters and changes shape. When something goes wrong that the employee didn't think was his responsibility, sure enough, someone points it out on the amoeba.

# Three Common
# Fields of Play

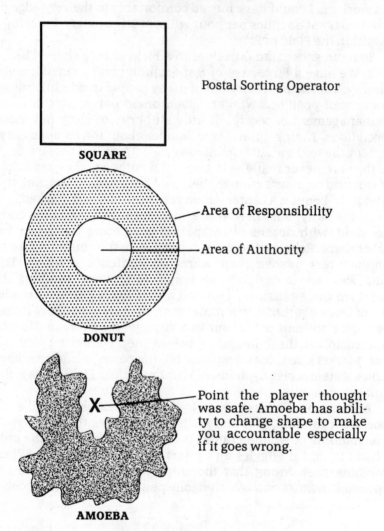

Postal Sorting Operator

**SQUARE**

Area of Responsibility

Area of Authority

**DONUT**

X— Point the player thought was safe. Amoeba has ability to change shape to make you accountable especially if it goes wrong.

**AMOEBA**

### Three Common Fields of Play

Great managers seek to minimize uncertainty, reducing the fear it produces.

Now, the main benefit to the square is that it decreases uncertainty. It creates common expectations. The only real problem with the square is that it has a top, a cap on it, a lid. If we were to take the lid off of the square and provide a growth outlet, then I believe we would have a perfect Field of Play for business. Following is a diagram of the business Field of Play.

## Western Leadership Group, Inc.

# Field of Play©

# Pay Dirt

|                          | Goal Line |                          |
|--------------------------|-----------|--------------------------|
| 1                        | 2         | 3                        |

*Out of Bounds Terminal*

# G.O.M.B.

*Out of Bounds Operational*

**Minimum Performance Standard**

# Safety Zone

**Humble Player—Helpful Coach**
*The End Line*

*Out of Bounds Performance*

## The Business Field of Play

The first element in defining what the Field of Play is and what you can do in it is to define what it is not, and to identify those things which are off the field, or those behaviors which are inappropriate and unacceptable. When a tennis ball hits beyond the line it's called out. When you hit a golf ball beyond the white stakes, it's out of bounds. When a wide receiver catches a football with one foot out of bounds, the official waves the pass incomplete. When a baseball goes to the left of third base it is a foul ball. In our business organizations we have certain behaviors that are not acceptable. Too often the out–of–bounds markers, however, are not clearly defined. Most businesses tend to be vague in this area.

One time I was working with a fast food company that had seven outlets. In the middle of a discussion of fear and expectations I turned to one of the managers and said, "Dave, do you have any fear in this company?" and he said,

"Oh, we've got a bunch of it."

"What are you afraid of?" I asked.

"I'm afraid of being fired."

It got rather hushed in the room because the owner and president was there with the supervisory staff and administrative people. I was prompted to ask,

"Dave, since you're afraid of being fired, tell me one thing that you know if you were doing you'd be gone."

He thought for a moment, then said, "I don't know."

Think about it. *An individual in almost constant fear who did not know what would get him fired.*

It seemed like a good idea to persist in the questioning. I asked the same question of the next manager and received the same response. All the managers had the same fear. I take my hat off to the president and owner of that company who sat silently, taking a rather bitter pill. As I met with him later in an individual conference, he relayed his astonishment that he had not been more aware of his managers' fear of losing their jobs. I assured him that his was not an unusual situation and suggested that we correct it by listing those behaviors the owner felt were serious enough to justify terminating a relationship.

At the next meeting with the managers, the 18–point list was passed around among the managers. The room was silent as the managers read the list with great interest. Then, one by one, sighs began to come forth from each of the participants, and David, our first manager, summed it up far better, I think, than anyone else when he said, "But I'm not doing any of these things."

To which the president responded, "Then, David, you have nothing to worry about."

## Western Leadership Group, Inc.
# REASONS FOR TERMINATION FROM RESTAURANT COMPANY

1. Failure to achieve known company goals.

2. Failure to achieve sales and profit objectives for thirteen consecutive weeks.

3. Failure to achieve mutually agreed upon goals as set out in writing.

4. Lying—caught telling an untruth.

5. Failure to protect lives of customers, employees or security of physical plant—doors, safes, fires due to negligence.

6. Failure to schedule the recommended number of man-hours.

7. Insubordination.

8. Fighting with or assaulting customer or fellow employees.

9. An obvious act of discrimination against another employee.

10. Offensive personal habits.
    a. vulgar language
    b. behavior unbecoming a manager

11. Failure to report for work without proper notification and authorization.

12. Failure to achieve tracking reports on time.

13. Purchasing from purveyors for personal use is forbidden.

14. Failure to achieve turnover goals.

15. Failure to account for cash shortage.

16. Allowing cash in unit to exceed $2,000.

17. Dishonesty in any form.

18. Any violation of state, municipal or federal law while on company premises.

What a great example of eliminating fear in an operation. What a great example of letting people know where the boundaries are, because when those boundaries are not clearly defined, there are two choices. To either flirt with danger and accept the resulting anxiety level, or to restrict behavior and stay far enough away from where the boundaries might be, allowing very little room to operate and succeed.

So the first step in the construction of the Field of Play agreement is to get those terminal out-of-bounds markers established, those things which result in termination of the agreement.

When you go to the city park to play ball, the first thing you do is establish the boundaries for the Field of Play. Then you set the goals within that Field of Play. The businesses in the home computer industry tried to set goals before they outlined the Field of Play. Many businesses are guilty of the same mistake, and the results can be disastrous.

A great manager constantly seeks to minimize uncertainty by clearly defining the Field of Play. A good manager clearly lays out the Field of Play agreement for each new employee, or each time an employee is given a new assignment. Only with these guidelines or management directives can an employee know how to act appropriately. Only when I know that somebody is not going to jerk the rug out from under me can I use a foundation of certainty as a springboard to get things done. Freedom is greatest when the boundaries are clearly defined. See the end of this chapter for some sample Field of Play agreements.

Once the out-of-bounds markers are clearly defined—the terminal area to the left hand side of the field and the operational area to the right hand side—the next step is to divide the field with hash marks into thirds. These represent the three most specific measurable Results to Resource Ratios for which the player is held accountable. If the player were Tony Dorsett he would be evaluated on carries per game, yards per carry and probably his receptions per game or yards per reception. Tony understands what is expected of him. With this Field of Play in place, the Dallas coaches can set realistic, mutually understood expectations for Tony.

The Dallas coaches know they win over 80% of their games when Tony gains more than 100 yards per game on the ground. You can see how an individual plan for one player fits into a bigger plan for team victories. How these are developed is covered in the following chapter.

Each Results to Resource Ratio in the Field of Play has three numerical levels. The most important is the minimum performance standard (MPS). As long as the player is playing above the minumum performance standard he is termed to be on the Field of Play and is in the game zone, which translates to, "Get off my back." The coach will not overcorrect, oversupervise or be picking the fly specks out of the pepper. The player's performance is proof of his capability to be self–determined, and players like this relationship.

The player finds himself in the second level if his performance drops below the minimum performance standard. There, he is like a quarterback retreating into his own end zone with the ball. If he does not get the ball out of there, he is going to be sacked. The referee will put his hands over his head and signal two points for the opposing team. It's not the end of the game, and perhaps not a critical situation, but it's not good. It's called a safety.

In our Field of Play agreement, we call that area the safety zone, but it is not a place where things are all that safe. The two h's apply. We have a *humble* player who admits that his performance has slipped below the predetermined minimum performance standard. He is coachable. Second, we have a coach who is *helpful,* who is committed to getting the player headed in the right direction, out of the safety zone and back onto the main playing field.

At the bottom of the safety zone is the end line. The player and the coach both know from their agreement before the game that any player going beyond that line is out of the game. It may not signal the removal of the player from the team, but may require that he or she be transferred to a new area of responsibility. In either case the power of this Field of Play agreement is the power of mutual expectation and mutual agreement.

The third level of performance, found at the other end of the Field of Play, is the pay dirt, where the player receives those special levels of compensation or special privileges that are extended to those who turn in superlative performances.

As we negotiate the Field of Play agreement between the player and the coach we establish a clearly defined Field of Play where, through the application of the Results to Resource Ratios, the player determines his or her own position on the field.

The play is monitored by scorecards that keep track of the resources and results, allowing the manager to assess and review the player's growth and accomplishments at a glance in periodic evaluations.

In addition, the coach must provide for the player an expectancy statement covering those areas which are not out–of–bounds but may not be immediately or specifically measurable. This is where the coach communicates his idiosyncrasies, attitudes, habits, specific areas of tenderness or specific areas of desired special emphasis.

Again, the writing down of all these parameters in a Field of Play agreement makes it possible for the coach and the player to understand where they need to agree, where they have started and where they eventually intend to end up. See Field of Play Expectations and Up Front Contract Expectations samples at end of chapter.

# Western Leadership Group, Inc.

# FIELD OF PLAY
# AGREEMENT

Between

Coach_____ Position_____
and_____ Position_____

**1st Meeting**  Date_____ Coach_____ Player _____

**2nd Meeting**  Date_____ Coach_____ Player_____

**3rd Meeting**  Date_____ Coach_____ Player_____

**1st Monthly
Meeting**  Date_____ Coach_____ Player_____

The Field of Play agreement, when assembled by use of the development agenda outlined later, represents the most significant agreement document available in American business today. It can be updated each month or more often if performance or lack thereof warrants it. It is simple. It is straightforward. It is specific and most of all, it is effective. It is the single most important instrument in accomplishing management by measurement in a professionally run organization.

### Field of Play Development Agenda

The Dallas Cowboys have over a hundred pages in their playbook—68 different plays, 35 different formations, 27 variations to each formation. It's all written down for every player to learn. When the quarterback yells, "Red, right, 34, 67, 2," everybody on the team knows exactly what to do. The Field of Play was laid out clearly ahead of time. The uncertainty is minimized. Performance is maximized.

A well thought out and firmly established Field of Play adds consistency to the game. The scampering here and there is minimized when there is a well thought out, written plan.

John Riggins, running back for the Washington Redskins, carried the ball 38 times in the 1983 Super Bowl. Averaging only four yards a carry he picked up 160 total yards. That consistency destroyed Miami. Woody Hays built Ohio State into a national powerhouse on three yards and a cloud of dust. LaVell Edwards at BYU has developed such consistency in passing that his opponents expect a pass when BYU has the ball second and goal on the one–yard line.

Some people are screamers. When something doesn't go their way they start yelling. Screaming isn't necessary when the Field of Play is clearly defined and everybody knows where the boundaries are.

A clearly outlined Field of Play results in certainty and consistency. And only after the Field of Play is established can realistic goals be set. You need to know where the field is before you can set the goals. In recreation we start with a clear definition of the boundaries, and establish goals within those boundaries. In business, many times we start by establishing goals without first having the boundaries. That's why it's often difficult to know if goals are realistic or not. The boundaries must precede the placement of goals in business as well as in sports.

To be an effective coach obviously requires more than creating a play book and a file cabinet full of Field of Play agreements. You must dedicate time to coaching.

The most effective way to implement the Field of Play agreement is with a one hour one–on–one uninterrupted coaching session with each player every month. Every month. If you are employing someone on a 40–hour week, or 173 hours a month, it isn't too much to ask that less than 1% of their time be earmarked for specific direction.

I know we give orders and instructions. We have staff meetings and team meetings and meetings to plan meetings. But I am talking here about coaching sessions, one–on–one, bare knuckles, quality time taken with each individual player.

No coach would want to enter a critical game, part of a championship series, and have someone say, "Sorry, coach, you can't have any timeouts, no half–time with the players, no time between quarters." No coach would accept that, yet in business we seem perfectly willing to accept job descriptions with annual or semi–annual review sessions.

You must come to the realization that feedback can never become too frequent, as long as it is honest and positive. Create a schedule so that your players know in advance when their hour arrives. If your span of control is too large for you to give this kind of quality coaching, spin off some of your people and build a second level of management. Get some assistant coaches. But do not hang onto a system that does not allow feedback from your people. That monthly review session can be conducted with the following agenda as a guide. After the agenda is a useful form for listing 30–day priorities to achieve project goals as well as the process goals which are measured on the Field of Play agreement. If you would like to receive a copy of a completed Field of Play agreement for your use, please send a stamped (two ounces of postage) 9x12 self–addressed envelope to The Game of Work, c/o Western Leadership Group, 180 East 2100 South, Suite 203, Salt Lake City, Utah 84115.

*One of the biggest problems in business today is people are not being told what is expected of them.* Every person has the right to personal freedoms and self–determination, but to get the job done––in sports as well as in business––somebody has to stand up and say, "This is what we are going to do, folks, and this is how we are going to do it."

In the absence of a clearly defined Field of Play, uncertainty thrives and performance suffers.

Western Leadership Group, Inc.

# FIELD OF PLAY
# DEVELOPMENT AGENDA

### Recommendations

1. Build a Field of Play folder for each Agreement (1 copy to coach and player)

    A.    Schematic of Field of Play
    B.    Expectancy statements from player and coach
    C.    Support commitments to player from coach
    D.    3 graphs on areas of measurable performance
    E.    Out of Bounds statements—Terminal and Operational

2. All meetings must be completed in no more than four weeks.

3. Each team member negotiates his/her agreement as a player before initiating any agreements as a coach.

### First Meeting

*Date Completed*

_____ 1. Coach establishes Out of Bounds
          A. *Terminal*
             1. Company wide
             2. Individual applications

          B. *Operational*

_____ 2. Coach suggests three areas for measurement (i.e., sales per day, average order, gross profit per deal).

_____ 3. Coach completes expectancy statement for the player. (Will include all responsibilities not measured as stated above.)

### Second Meeting
(To be held within 7 days of first meeting)

*Date Completed*

_____ 1. Player suggests additional areas for measurement. (If agreed to by player and coach, these replace areas suggested by coach.)

103

_____   2. Player *suggests* minimum performance standards and "end line levels" for these areas of measurement.

_____   3. Player provides his expectancy statement. (Must correlate with the 5 year plan.)

_____   4. Player requests support commitment from coach.

_____   5. Player suggests pay dirt levels and desired rewards.

### Third Meeting
(To be completed within 7 days of second meeting)

*Date Completed*

_____   1. Negotiation and agreement on all performance areas.

_____   2. Review graph quadrants and agree on frequency of reporting.

_____   3. Sign final agreements.

### Fourth Meeting
(and continued meetings)
(First fourth meeting to be completed within 30 days of third meeting)

*Date Completed*

_____   A. Complete Review Agenda

_____   B. Monthly Plan
1. Player comes to meeting with Monthly Plan completed to review with his coach.

2. Player will have entered seven items he feels need to be accomplished in next 30 days, in order of his suggested priority.

3. Player and coach derive from seven items a negotiated list of 5 priorities for the next 30 days.

4. These meetings are also used for quarterly and annual review as compared to 15 month and 60 month plans.

Western Leadership Group, Inc.

# FIELD OF PLAY REVIEW SESSIONS
# AGENDA

I.   Player Reviews Successes
   A. Graph
   B. Success 30 days program

II.  Player Self-Analysis
   A. Present—7 most important goals
      Last 30 days goals
   B. Future days—7 most important goals
      Next 30 days goals

III. Coach Has Discussion of Next 30 Day Priorities
   A. Review top priorities
   B. Prepare final Prioritized List in triplicate
      1. Coach
      2. Player
      3. Field of Play File

IV.  15 Month Review—If Quarterly Meeting

V.   5 Year Review—If Annual Meeting

VI.  Personal Counseling

## Western Leadership Group, Inc.

# FIELD OF PLAY
# MONTHLY PLAN

---
*Deadline Date*

### 30 Day Priorities

1.

2.

3.

4.

5.

6.

7.

*Directions:*
    Be specific.
    State goals in "done" sense rather than "doing."

    1 copy to Player
    1 copy to Coach
    1 copy to Contract File

## Western Leadership Group, Inc.

# FIELD OF PLAY EXPECTATIONS
# FROM HIS COACH

1. Have a career orientation.

2. Be a conscientious counselor.

3. Support the performer.

4. Be positive and specific.

5. Write all unresolved questions at least weekly and send to me.

6. Expect growth through new tasks and assignments and techniques. Admit self-imposed limitations and attack past conditioning daily.

7. 110% support especially in front of members of the W.L.G. team.

8. Negatives come up. Positives go down.

9. Be a product of the product.
     Personal goals program with visuals board and affirmations tape current, up-to-date and worthy to be demonstrated.

10. Expect and use "why" communication—if not provided, ask.

11. Trust coach's motives to have your best interests at heart.

## Western Leadership Group, Inc.
# UP FRONT CONTRACT
# FIELD OF PLAY

### Terminal Out of Bounds

Because our business is built on trust and respect for our integrity and professionalism, we must be above reproach. Therefore, those things which will result in a member of W.L.G., Inc. being subject to immediate termination of employment if engaged in are:

1. Embezzlement or theft; any misappropriation of money due to W.L.G., Inc.; misappropriations of supplies, inventories or trade secrets.

2. Any violation of copyrights held by SMI, W.L.G., Inc., its principals or any other supplier of material which may result in endangering our franchise or distributorship agreement.

3. Failure to perform a service for which we have been contracted or been paid.

4. Using W.L.G., Inc. representation or the contacts you have made as a result of your employment, or developed expertise, to perform any service like or similar to our services which is not billed through the company.

5. Lying or any misrepresentation of the facts concerning status of a sale, an account receivable, or the whereabouts or behavior of self or a fellow employee.

6. Failure to meet one sale per 44 working days (after the first ten sales have been achieved) or failure to achieve a sale within three times your career mean days between sales (after your MDBS has been established through the first ten sales).

7. Any adultery or fornication or immoral relationship with a W.L.G., Inc. employee, or an employee of any of our client companies.

8. Disorderly behavior which is alcohol or drug induced in the presence of a client; whether you are working or socializing, or are observed by the client.

9. Any declaration to another individual(s) which is disloyal, degrading, or defamatory of the company, its officers, or employees.

10. Failure to treat any employee, client employee, or client as an individual and member of the species created above all.

11. Any behavior, public or private, which detracts from the ethical and professional reputation of Western Leadership Group, Inc.

### Disciplinary Out of Bounds

1. Failure to attend two consecutive regularly scheduled sales training meetings without approval from the sales manager or officer of Western Leadership Group.

Revised and Effective 10/1/82
Read and Received: _____

Approved: _____
Signed: _____

# Results to Resource Ratio

*If winning isn't important, why do we spend all that money on scoreboards?*

—Chuck Coonradt

In business one of the most effective measurement devices is return on investment. It may be expressed in several ways: return on assets, return on equity, return on net capital invested, return on net assets. Return on investment measures the amount of profitability one can generate with certain assets, be they inventory, people, cash, plant and/or equipment. We do very well in utilizing this measurement in a macro sense, or on an overall company level. We look at it annually. It's always in the annual report. And we may even evaluate it quarterly, seldom more frequently than that.

There is a parallel in recreation and sports. We use the term Results to Resource Ratio, or the RRR. In athletics, baseball for example, there are several Results to Resource Ratios. Batting championships are decided on the batting average. The relationship between the number of at bats (resource) and the number of hits (results). The RRR for a league leader will be in the high .300's, perhaps over .375. The greatest baseball batter in history by this measurement was Ted Williams, who batted .400 for an entire season. Batting average is an RRR.

In football we have an RRR ratio for practically every member of the team. Offensive line coaches rate their players' performance on the number of times the block is effectively held long enough to permit the play to develop, be it a pass blocking assignment or a running block. The number of opportunities or the number of plays in which a lineman blocks versus the number of times he holds the block for the required number of seconds reflect that RRR.

As we move into what are called the skill positions, those which come in contact with the ball, we have an even larger number of Results to Resource Ratios. Receiver performance is measured in total receptions, receptions per game, yards per reception or game, number of games over a hundred yards, total yardage for the season. In fact, in all sports huge computer memory banks constantly measure results to resources for all of the players, and generate beautiful television computer graphics in explaining those numbers to the fans.

In golf, the money becomes the most important measurement. Everybody knows how much the top golfers earn. The IRS loves professional golfers. But along with that we have expanded RRR's, including average strokes per round. We have a driving percentage, which is the number of drives placed in the fairway; the approach percentage, which is the number of approaches effectively delivered to the green from within 200 yards. We have a putting percentage, or putts per round. These RRR's are measured in one–hundredths of strokes even though the smallest increment of measurement in golf is one stroke. The experts recognize that if you put together all of the measured elements of the game consistently, with the right timing you will come away with a victory.

The Results to Resource Ratio, then, is also essential in effectively executing the management function. It's the key relationship between the stockholders and the management team. It's also predominant in sports. We must ask ourselves two questions: Why is it necessary? And why has it not been expanded further into management circles?

The answer to the first question is both simple and complex. The first reason for wanting an RRR ratio is to find out how much you are going to get paid. In the stock market the price–earnings ratio and the ability of one management team to generate substantial amounts of profit with reduced commitments of assets makes their stock the glamour issue of the day. Less efficient management teams who require more employed assets are going to be less attractive in the investment field.

You find a parallel in sports when you consider the win record of the Dallas Cowboys is over 80% when Tony Dorsett achieves over 100 yards per game. That's why Tony Dorsett makes so much money.

Why is the Results to Resource Ratio so important in professional sports? Because the amount of money a professional athlete gets paid is a direct result of his RRR's. Improving the RRR's means more money.

Then why, in the American workforce, have we failed to generate sufficient RRR's? There are two reasons. One, we have never understood the obvious importance of the RRR's. Two, we have never defined the fundamental way in which they are put together. Therefore, managers are inhibited or intimidated by this process. Let's set forth the method for constructing an RRR in your firm or department.

Divide a sheet of paper with one vertical line as in the diagram below. At the top of one area write "Resources." At the top of the other area write "Results." For this example let's use a controller in a medium–size organization who has a staff responsible for all the fundamental management accounting reports, payroll, accounts payable, accounts receivable, etc. It might be easier to look at a mail sorter, salesperson or lathe operator––but if we can do it for a controller, we can do it for anybody.

Now we may ask ourselves initially what are his resources. Some of the words come easily: time, subordinates, know–how, equipment, calculators, electronic typewriters, word processors. He also has a resource of space occupied by administrative people, space which cannot be assigned to sales or manufacturing or to the productivity side of the business.

### Results to Resource Ratio

| Resource | Results |
|---|---|
| Time: | |
| Man–hours | |
| Minutes | |

We must ask ourselves one major question that runs throughout *The Game of Work*, one that involves the key ingredient in motivation in recreation: How do I measure the ingredients? When I write down "time," how do I measure it?

The easiest way, of course, is in hours and minutes. And so below "time" I write down the amount of time this individual has available to him––40 or 48 hours a week. As a footnote, we may take the amount of time that he feels productive, the time he real-ly feels he has to manage. (If you were measuring the time resource of an entrepreneur, you may pick the number of hours he spends away from his family.)

Now we go to subordinates' time. Again, it is measured in at least two ways. One is the man–hours. You may look at an employee and write down his total departmental man–hours based on a 40–hour week, 4.3 weeks in a month, or 172 hours times the number of people on the staff. With a five–person department, he would have in excess of 800 hours plus the controller's hours on a monthly basis. A second way to measure the labor resource is in dollars of labor cost. We're beginning to define our resource.

Now, the machine time. We may look at that in dollars or in hours. We might look at the entire budget, including man–hours, space and time in terms of an overall dollar cost for the business or any particular department.

As the manager begins to define resources, something becomes very apparent: that resources in most organizations are easier to define than results. Selecting the right results is the essence of effective management by measurement.

| Resource | Results |
| --- | --- |
| Time—800 man–hours | |
| Space—1500 sq. ft | |
| Equipment—$7,000/mo. | |

Let's take the same approach on the right side of the chart. What results are we looking for from the controller? If you look at his job description, or the understanding he obtained in Accounting 101 in college, we will find words like: provide management with *timely, accurate, and complete* financial information to *profitably* conduct the affairs of the business organization.

Now, let's list each of the desired results: timely, accurate and complete reporting (see chart). Behind each of these results we write a method of measuring them. If we are looking for accuracy, we might look at a percentage error factor. If we are looking for timeliness, we might look at a variance between when reports were promised and when they were delivered. If we're looking for completeness, we can use either of the two previous statements.

| Resource | Results |
|---|---|
| Timely–– | Difference between regular project promise dates and delivery dates. |
| Accuracy–– | a) Errors per number of items prepared. |
| | b) Number of times a report must be prepared to be accurate. |
| Profit–– | a) Net profit for entire company. |
| | b) Net or gross profit generated by an individual department. |

Now we want to identify the most expensive resource and the most valuable result and see if they can be combined. For example, we might look at this controller and his staff and conclude that the human element is, in fact, the most expensive resource we have. So let's underline or circle that on the left–hand side of our chart. Next we'll go to the result side and ask ourselves the same question. What is our most valuable result? We might look, even though the controller is not in total control, at profit as the most important result we're looking for. We can then construct a preliminary ratio of net profit dollars per total department man–hours. *Net profit dollars per total department man–hours.*

| Resource | Results |
|---|---|
| (People) | Timely |
| Space | Accurate |
| Equipment | (Profit) |

Net Profit per Employee Man–hour

1 2 3 4 5 6 7 8 9 10 11 12 13 14 15 Periods

When you come up with a new RRR that becomes a measurement of someone's productivity or output, the questions invariably pop up. What does it mean? Even if we looked at it and found out what it said, what would it really mean? Is it worthwhile to keep track of it? We've never done this before. What are the measurements? Where do they go? Well, we recognize as managers that a number one priority is to minimize the uncertainty on our team.

So, having constructed a new look, we must first expect to encounter some resistance. If we are able to do our research in such a fashion that we can look at historical data and assemble it in new terms before we necessarily expose our players to the information, we then have a tremendous opportunity to tell them what it means and reduce the fear and apprehension quickly.

For example, one of our service organization clients recently went back and identified their net income per employee hour for the last five years. They found improvement in the ratio from year to year of the following magnitudes:

### Productivity Improvement Chart

|                          | '79 | '80 | '81 | '82 | '83 |
|--------------------------|-----|-----|-----|-----|-----|
| Profit increases         | 31% | 27% | 15% | 11% | 4%  |
| Wage increases           | 9%  | 11% | 14% | 17% | 18% |
| Net gain in productivity per dollar paid | 22% | 18% | 1% | (6%) | (14%) |

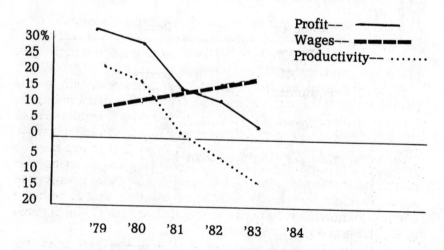

114

You can see some trends developing which are dangerous. With this historical perspective, the chairman of the board committed the human resources man to provide a plan for subsequent staffing, not based on opinion, observation or judgment, but on a measurement of a Results to Resource Ratio.

The important concept here is to get the RRR to reflect accurately the philosophies and intent of the organization. For example, we might conclude that in a typical growing, developing organization, after the initial adding of computers and personnel to the accounting department, the relationship between total accounting department expenses and sales would begin to decline. Procedures would become routine as the company begins to grow. After all, it takes only a marginally greater amount of time to process twice the number of invoices. The input times are not doubled for orders that are twice as big. We only need one vice–president controller. We will tend to fill in with lower wage–scale people. Our average hourly rate should come down with the passing of time. And so I think we could make a case for the fact that the RRR we call sales per administrative man–hour might be expected to rise over time.

It is my favorite betting position that in any company you have ever been affiliated with, if you track it over a ten–year period, we'll find that without measurement by management those costs have in fact not decreased but increased. And that the sales per administrative hour has gone down over a period of time in spite of inflationary pressure to increase prices. We are, in most instances, doing less work with more people today than we were 10 years ago.

If the computer is justifiable––reducing turn–around time and making a contribution to the organization over the cost of that computer––there should be a real savings when you add the cost of the new resource to the resource side of our chart.

Before you accuse me of unrelenting conservativism, let me point out that it is not our purpose in *The Game of Work* to impose a will or a direction. If you wish to increase your administrative costs as a percentage of sales, that's your business and your right. The point being made in *The Game of Work* is that you need to know what is happening, know if you are winning or losing. Our point is that management must provide the worker or supervisor with a realistic and clearly defined expectation so that he has a chance of knowing whether he is winning or losing. The purpose of the RRR is to do that very thing.

Included in the concept of a RRR is the *per*. Sales *per* man–hour. Yards *per* game. Yards *per* carry. The *per* is the measurement tool that you see throughout *The Game of Work*. It triggers the relationship between results and resources.

Every professional has them. Every member of my management team has them. Every member of yours will want to develop them.

A word of caution. The concept of measurement is sometimes regarded as punitive and must therefore be approached carefully and sold to the players as a benefit.

When a salesman is in trouble he has to call home more often and report more frequently. Or consider a business situation where things are not going well and they call in the auditors, who count clearly and frequently and persist in this behavior modification mode until we get it fixed. Once it is fixed, almost denying the power of measurement and frequent feedback, the auditors leave and take the measurement system with them, and we are again left on our own with less feedback than we had when we were in the problem mode, somehow feeling that we should continue to muddle through until it goes bad, knowing that the auditors will return.

Don't take me wrong. Auditors are some of my best friends. But we do, I believe, raise our generations of management people with a certain predisposed apprehension towards measurement. Therefore, selling a measurement system or concept is imperative.

How do you gain a commitment to measurability? How do you reach inside and turn that switch on? We'll discuss that more in the chapter on motivation, but let me suggest that there are some levels of involvement that can be developed.

We mentioned earlier the advantage of a historical perspective. Take, for example, an accountant's receivables. It is easy to go back and create a 24–month time line showing the pattern of days of sales outstanding. We've done that in a number of organizations.

Following is a chart of accounts receivables for a company.

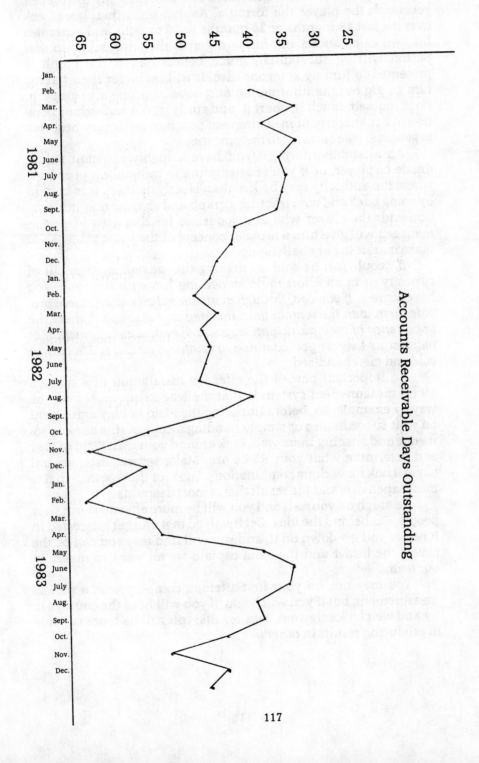

If the information is generated and processed by the player, you teach the player the formula. As that individual goes back over the last 18 months or 24 months or 36 months and generates his own calculations and his own graph, the impression on that person will be substantial, much better than if the graph is presented to him by someone else. It will be better than having him go dig out the information and have someone else graph it. Do it yourself, touch it, chart it, and study it. The self–administration of a management measurement program is the very best way to generate commitment to the process.

An alternative form, if you have a highly resistant subordinate or player, or if you're attempting to influence a peer level where the authority may be less than clearly defined, is to benefit by going back and constructing a graph and sharing that information with the player who is responsible for that area of performance. It will give him a broader concept of the point you wish to make in training or challenging.

If people can be sold on making that adventure trip, out of curiosity or in an effort to do something fun with their job, you have scored. *If you can, through motivational communication, provide them with the why in your thinking and share with them the importance of their participation, you will have a commitment that will last as long as you continue to reinforce it.* The RRR's can be sold and merchandised.

An important part of the effective installation of a management measurement system is that the leadership must lead the way by example. So, before imposing the Field of Play agreement on your subordinates or simply handing a copy of this book to someone and wishing them well, look around your own Field of Play and determine what your RRR's are. Make several lists, several pages. Look for various combinations. Look for the resource that is most expensive, and the result that is most desirable.

Be tough on yourself and you will be more effective with your people. Get behind the idea. Get involved in it and get interested in it before you get down on it, and you will find that you can be the coach, the leader and the team captain we all want so much on our team.

You may not, on your first attempt, come up with a perfect measurement, but if you will begin, if you will have the courage to try and watch closely your own results, you will be more capable in producing results in others.

# Picking Winners

*Freedom is greatest when the boundaries are clearly defined.*
*--Chuck Coonradt*

Every year before the NFL draft begins the teams have lots of data to study, four years of college playing statistics and scouting reports that may go as far back as high school. They have numerous personal observations to back up the numerical data.

In business, most of us do not have that kind of information to help us pick winners for our team. It's easy to pay a Magic Johnson a million dollars after he has proven himself, but it's a lot tougher to snatch a Moses Malone out of a New Jersey high school and give him a lot of money in the expectation that ten years down the road he'll become a star center. In business, we interview Viet Nam veterans and ex-college protestors who have the capability to starve for us like Rocky Blier did for the Pittsburgh Steelers.

Look for the numbers, not the number of schools where they had their ticket punched. Look for results, the candidate's track record in similar positions.

In sports they always check the numbers. When a baseball club trades pitchers for hitters, or fielders for coaches, they don't worry about personality, or who the guy went to high school with. They care about performance, statistics. The key to picking winners is to get as close to the attributes we listed in the chapter on winning as possible, plus the following. When you can't get numbers, you look for heart. And how do you do that?

First, a winner believes in himself or herself and sees a relationship between past accomplishments and the future assignment. They can't have this if their future assignment isn't clearly spelled out. Good feelings about past success must be transferred to the new assignment.

Sometimes a wise manager may recognize qualities in a recruit beyond what the new employee can see in himself. The coach of a Super Bowl team once said, "Coaching is merely taking them someplace they don't think they can go on their own."

As a general rule, your most likely winner is the person who can find a direct relationship or connection between past success and the new assignment. By the time some successful college basketball players reach the NCAA final four, they have only lost a dozen games in their careers, since grade school. You wouldn't hire a talented offensive lineman to play quarterback. You want someone who has had success that can be associated with the new assignment.

Second, winners have commitment to the team's direction. They see a direct relationship between the company's team goals and their own individual goals. In sports this is the player who can see a relationship between the hours and hours of practice and the few moments of glory, and recognize that as a bargain.

Third, you're looking for coachability. For every recognized winner there is a coach in the background. Winners recognize there is knowledge and information beyond their own capabilities, and they are willing to assimilate through the coach. They are open to the leadership of others. The great ones have mentors.

There are several excellent books on the interviewing process. I won't attempt to override that great body of knowledge in a few short lines, but let me emphasize that the hiring process must be the beginning of a coach–winner relationship. The great coaches are those who constantly seek to minimize uncertainty, and that begins in the hiring process where you establish the Field of Play.

Many business managers when indoctrinating a new employee have no concept of what it means to set up the Field of Play. They go through meaningless routines, like going over the new person's resume'.

"So you worked at Ford Motor Company. How're they doing?"

"You went to Clayton Valley High School. Did you know Bill Nelson? Class of '70 too, I believe."

How many business managers waste time reading back the resume' to a new employee as if the kid didn't know what was on it, or like the new boss is trying to catch the kid in a lie.

At my Western Leadership company where we conduct management efficiency and productivity seminars, the Field of Play interview goes something like this. (Once the individual is hired it really isn't important to me that he worked for Ford Motor Company or knew Bill Nelson in high school.)

"John, here's what I've got to have done," I begin. "As a member of our marketing staff I expect you to do whatever you have to do to get one of our senior staff people in front of a chief executive officer in a closing situation at least once every five working days. And here's how we're going to calculate that. We have in our company what we call 'mean length of time between closing presentations' and I'm going to show you how to start tracking that. Your first goal is to go out and get one. I don't know if that will take a week or a month, but get one. The second goal is to get the second in less time than it took for the first. Your third goal is to get the third in less time than the average of the first two. Your fourth goal is to continue to beat your average."

This is the performance formula I use to start new salesmen. I have helped other companies adopt variations of this formula. I know of no other Field of Play that has worked better in getting new salesmen working productively. After explaining what is expected, I tell the salesperson I expect him or her to chart their progress on a chart similar to the one on the following page.

I tell the new employee what some of the best and worst performances were by other employees, then ask him if he will perform in the Field of Play I have outlined.

I make it clear that performance will be evaluated on how well he performs within the guidelines, not on personality, charm, appearance, sex, race or how he did at Ford Motor Company or who he knew in high school.

Then I go into more detail on *how* to get those closing appointments. The number of contacts that will result in at least one opening presentation every day. How former employees have done, especially the best ones. When I'm finished the new person has a clear picture of the Field of Play, a way to measure his performance, the record book so he knows what to shoot for, and a clear understanding of my expectations. That's the way it is in sports, and that's the way it must be in every business.

When Tony Dorsett entered the Dallas Cowboys organization, they probably said something like the following to him:

"Tony, here's what we expect from you. You'll be carrying the ball from 20 to 35 times a game. We expect you to average close to five yards a carry. We also expect you to decoy and block on this

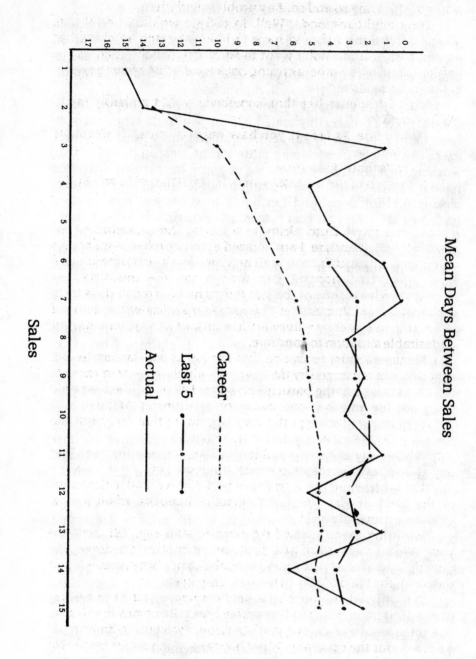

Days

Mean Days Between Sales

Sales

Career
Last 5
Actual

122

number of plays, and catch so many passes, and sit on the bench when we're doing so and so. Any problem with that?"

Tony might respond, "Well, in college we didn't do it that way. I don't think I should have to block or catch anything but screen passes, and I don't want to sit on the bench. Besides, I've talked to one of the other running backs and I think your expectations are unrealistic."

With a response like that, somebody would probably say to Tony,

"That's fine. As I see it, you have only got one of 27 decisions you need to make."

"What's that?" asks Tony.

"At which of the other 27 places in the NFL would you like to play next year?"

As you move from hiring to training, the commitment to specificity must endure. I am amazed at the number of managers who express dissatisfaction with an employee's performance and then when that hopeful day arrives for the unsatisfactory employee to leave, one of the last things he is asked to do is train the replacement. Incredible! The manager abdicates the reins of leadership to someone whose work is unsatisfactory, enabling an undesirable situation to continue.

Managers must recognize that the joy or satisfaction in any experience is measured by the degree to which it meets or exceeds the expectations of the participant. Missed or unfulfilled expectations are the number one cause of relationship failure. It is therefore imperative from the very beginning that you form the clearest possible expectations for an employee.

When I say earliest possible moment, I mean the very first day of work, even earlier in the recruiting process.

The athlete and the worker are both lost without a clear view of the Field of Play. Yet, what usually happens when a new employee comes aboard?

We bring them in the first morning and say, "Hi, how are you?" We sit them down at a desk and let another employee, frequently a mediocre performer, describe their sometimes warped picture of the Field of Play to the new employee.

Typically when you hire a new employee you have his undivided attention until the first coffee break. He comes in at 8 a.m. in a three piece suit, calling you Mr. Coonradt, eager to know what he can do for the company. What happens at the coffee break? He meets another employee, someone who's been around a long time and has a confused or warped picture of the Field of Play.

The new employee comes back from the coffee break with the

tie undone, the shirt sleeves rolled up, and it's "Chuck, baby. What's cookin'?" Too many managers turn over the leadership responsibilities to the wrong people, abdicate the coach's role, and then spend the rest of their supervisory time with that employee trying to keep him out of the terminal out–of–bounds area.

My recommendation is that when you hire a new person you don't let them out of your sight for the first 48 hours. Have them in all your meetings. Take them to lunch. Don't even let them go to the restroom unless you know they will be alone in there. There's only one chance for a first impression. Make sure new employees get a clear understanding of the correct Field of Play right from the beginning. It'll save a lot of problems later on and could even make the difference between a successful or a failing experience for an employee.

The need to establish control over a new employee and a correct picture right from the beginning is illustrated in what they do to your kid at summer camp. Right off the counselor will invite the 12 or 14 kids in a unit onto an open, grassy field to play "kill the counselor." The kids are invited to attack the counselor, all at once, and beat him up—on the surface just a good roughhouse activity. But what happens is that while collectively the kids are wearing down the counselor and will eventually have him pinned to the ground, individually each kid is feeling the counselor's power as he tosses kids here and there during the course of the battle. Each kid is feeling how strong the counselor is.

Four or five days later when one of those kids is goofing off in church, all the counselor has to do is reach over and grab the kid's arm. If the kid continues to misbehave, the counselor just squeezes a little harder until the kid remembers how easily the counselor tossed him about during the game. He settles down. Subtle, reserved authority is vastly superior to intimidating power.

What many managers don't realize is that how people respond in an organization, and how they assess the organization in their minds, is primarily dependent on their relationship with the person to whom they report. When an individual comes aboard, the manager is in the driver's seat receiving respect and appropriate responses from the new employee. That respect remains until expectations are not met. It's imperative that expectations be understood and clearly defined.

# Coaching Winners to Greatness

*All coaching is, is taking a player where he can't take himself.*
*--Bill McCartney, Defensive Coordinator*
*San Francisco '49ers*
*(Super Bowl Season)*

What is motivation? Drive, incentive, desire, go–power, something you need when you don't have it--like credit at the bank. Billions of dollars are spent on motivation every year. Look at all the pins, plaques, awards, prizes and, of course, the jackets and blazers--red, blue, white, black and gold. I've heard somewhere the Century 21 real estate franchise was started by a guy who needed to get rid of 15,000 gold blazers.

What is motivation? If you split this word in half the first word you have is "motive." And if you add one letter to the back half, you have "action." Motivation is a motive for action--a reason to do something.

## Motiv(e)/a(c)tion

Motivation is omnipresent. It's always present. It may be good, bad or have no morality at all, but it is always there. It's happening, or not happening, now. It's not something you can buy in a box or bottle and put on a shelf.

There is no such thing as an unmotivated person. The teenager who is too tired to mow the lawn on a Saturday afternoon is saving his energy for a shower and date. He is motivated, though not in the direction preferred by his parents. Nevertheless he is motivated. Everybody is motivated. Have you had a drink in

125

the last 24 hours? You were motivated by thirst to do so. Have you slept in the last 24 hours? You were motivated by weariness to do it.

The big question is how to get more of it, how to get ourselves and those around us more motivated in business and professional pursuits. In order to know how to get more of it, we must first understand how it works. There are three kinds of motivation.

Fear is the most common form of motivation. Parents use it on children, and bosses on workers all the time. When you have a donkey cart at the bottom of a hill, the fear motivator is the little man cracking the whip. Like most fear motivators he is sitting down. The theory is simple, but it doesn't always work, at least not as well as it should. Sometimes the donkey kicks back or sits down. If the hill is steep enough and the load heavy, the donkey gets to a point where he would rather take a beating than continue. People do that too.

Sometimes salesmen get to a point where they would rather sit in the office and starve than get out and work. Most offices have people who are starving to death. The best thing you can do for them is fire them. People are self–determined. You've got to let them do what they want to do. If they want to starve you can't stop them, but you don't need to pay them while they are doing it.

One of the big problems with fear motivation is that you need a guy with a whip to watch over every donkey. That's expensive. You have six guys sitting around doing the starving routine, so you kick one, and the other five say, "Yup, see how tough it is." But they still don't go out and do anything. And the human relations guy comes by and gets after you for kicking the guy. You can't win with fear.

The next alternative is to get a long stick, tie a carrot on the end, and hold it out in front of the donkey's nose. According to the theory, the donkey will look at the carrot and pull the wagon to the top of the hill. But there are five kinds of situations where the carrot won't work.

One is when the donkey is not hungry enough. Sometimes when you have a donkey that is content with 1,500 carrots a month and you put him in a job where he can earn 3,000 carrots a month, he'll slow down his performance to catch up with his expectations and needs. He's not hungry.

This happens frequently in the real estate industry. Take a guy who is used to earning $1,200 a month and make him a real estate salesman. His boss tells him to go out and get a new listing every three days. He does it. Then the boss makes the biggest mistake in the world. He sells a house for the new man, then compounds the mistake by taking the salesman to the closing and paying him a $3,000 commission, in one day. This usually happens his fourth or fifth week in the business. The salesman puts it in his checking account, which is now much bigger than his self–image. He can't get his self–image to go up, so he waits for his checking account to go down.

The second situation where a carrot won't work is when the carrot isn't big enough. The donkey looks at the carrot, then back at the load in the cart, then at the steepness of the hill, and thinks, "If you think I'm going to pull this load up that hill for one lousy carrot...."

The third problem with carrots occurs when the road is too steep. You cannot ask people to do more than they are able. Sometimes taking a class, learning new skills, or gaining more product knowledge will change the situation.

Fourth, carrots won't work when the load is too heavy. This occurs when somebody says, "I know I can make a lot of money in this business, but do you know how many people I have to call on to make a sale?"

The fifth I discovered quite by surprise. I was giving a lecture on motivation and this little lady in the back stands up and asks, "Chuck, what do you do if the donkey doesn't like carrots?" As loose as I am, I wasn't prepared for that question. It stopped me dead in my tracks and I started thinking about it.

It occurred to me that that lady had put me onto one of the fundamental problems of incentive motivation. Not long after that experience I was sitting in the back row at a sales meeting when the vice–president of the company showed the salesmen a beautiful 25–inch console television in a white plastic case, an ultra–modern Star Wars look. It was to be presented to the top salesman that month.

I was sitting next to two salesmen who had been around a long time. One of them poked the other and said, "Big deal, it's worth maybe $700. If I got it my wife would spend $2,700 to redo the family room just to make the decor right again." The guy thought that $700 carrot would cost him nearly $3,000 to accept. He didn't like the carrot.

Another bad carrot situation occurs when the executive says, "Work hard and we'll make you a manager."

The worker thinks, "Hmm, manager. That's somebody who works 30% longer hours for 10% less money with three times the heart attack rate and six times the divorce rate. I don't like your carrot." He'll slow down his performance just short of the prize. If you're going to use carrots, make sure the donkey likes them.

## Stop treating people like donkeys

Whereas donkeys may respond best to whips and carrots, people don't. People respond best to their own goals, if they have them. You don't need to treat people like donkeys if you understand goal striving. Reaching goals is a form of winning. People like to win. And winning is its own reward most of the time. People who are trying to win by reaching clearly defined goals don't necessarily need carrots or the whip. Winning is its own reward.

Remember, there is no such thing as an unmotivated person. Goal setting harnesses that motivation and channels it in the right direction. Through proper goal–setting techniques discussed in Chapter 3, a person's desires, wants and needs can be directed into purposeful activity.

The most effective form of motivation takes place when people are allowed to choose their own rewards, set their own goals and decide how they will accomplish those goals. People can be highly motivated in sports because they know nobody is going to change the rules or the boundaries in the middle of the game. An athlete can train and condition with all his heart, knowing the rules or boundaries are not going to change. In recreation the rules are clear by which I exchange my talents, abilities and energy for the things I want to have. Unfortunately this is frequently not the case in business, and that is why in most cases people will pay for the privilege of working harder than they will work when they are paid. Motivation then, the motive for action, is the trade between what I want and what I am willing to give for it.

Consider a balance beam, or a teeter–totter. Keep in mind that motivation is a *motive* for *action*. On the left side you have the weight or intensity of the *motive*. On the right side you have the weight or difficulty of the *action*.

**Example 1.** If I hold a .357 Magnum to your head, cock the hammer and ask you to call me Mr. Coonradt instead of Chuck, you will be motivated to obey, very quickly. A gun at the head is a strong *motive*, while calling me Mr. Coonradt is an easy *action*. The gun will motivate you to comply.

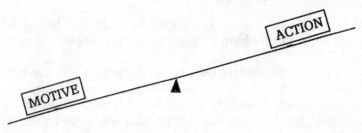

**Example 2.** If I handed you a quarter in an attempt to get you to run 10 miles with a 50–pound pack on your back, you would think I was crazy. In this case the *action* far outweighs the *motive*, so nothing happens. *The key to motivation is providing motives that outweigh the desired actions.*

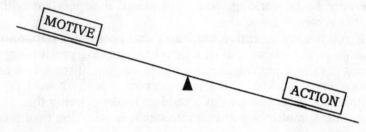

The relationship between *motive* and *action* is illustrated perfectly in a holdup that took place in the Old West. A homesteader and his wife were driving their wagon to town when a bandit jumped out of the bushes pointing a six–shooter at them and ordered the man to step down. He obeyed.

"Can you dance?" said the bandit to the man.

"No," responded the frightened farmer.

"We'll see," said the gunman. Then he fired three shots beneath the man's feet. The man danced and the outlaw laughed.

"Can your mule dance?" asked the gunman when the dust had settled.

"No," responded the frightened farmer.

"We'll see," said the gunman. Then he fired three shots beneath the poor animal's feet. The mule reared up and jerked the wagon about, frightening the woman. The outlaw laughed again, until the woman reached under the seat, pulled out a double–barrelled shotgun and pointed it at the gunman.

"Boy," she said. "Is that a six–shooter in your hand?"

"Yes, ma'am," said the startled outlaw, beginning to wish he were somewhere else, realizing he had fired all six shots.

"Son," she continued, "have you ever kissed the rear end of a mule?"

"No, ma'am," he said, looking up into the barrel of the shotgun, "but I'm looking forward to the privilege with great anticipation."

Whenever the motive outweighs the action you are going to get results. Everybody in the world has a balance beam in their head. Motivation is simply the process of piling things on the motive side until movement occurs and the action gets off the ground.

The bottom line in motivation is getting the balance beam to move. If you are a fear motivator and nothing is moving, you get a bigger whip. A shotgun at five feet is more effective than a BB pistol at 1,000 yards. The problem is application. You can kick a guy out of the office, but you can't be with him every minute to make sure he is working. You can't afford a supervisor with a whip to oversee every worker.

If you are an incentive motivator and nothing is happening, you get a bigger carrot. But in a time of shrinking profit margins you can't really afford bigger and bigger carrots. It would be nice to give everyone a $100,000 a year guarantee with 12 weeks paid vacation, but most companies would go broke offering that big a carrot. And sometimes you run into workers who don't want carrots.

So how do you get more motivation without investing in a bigger whip and more carrots?

I'll put it in a box for you. The key to successful motivation is individual involvement. That means tying the individual goals of your people to the goals of the business. To win in *The Game of Work*, you create a methodology where people and the business are closely linked to grow together with common or compatible goals. In order for this to happen, you must recognize the following:

### 1) WIIFM--What's in it for me?

A vital question every person has on his or her mind when coming to work each morning. Any time anybody runs into a new situation where they're going to be asked to perform, they've got this question: "What's in it for me?" Sometimes the question isn't verbalized because the employee doesn't want the boss to think he is selfish, a troublemaker or a bad employee. Still, the question is there and a smart manager will recognize it in the goal-setting process.

## 2) WSI--Why should I?

Children ask this question a lot, at least until they hear the non–answer "because I said so" so many times that they give up asking. Parents give this non–answer because they don't know or are too lazy to figure out the real answer. They would be better off saying, "I don't know."

*When someone asks you with their eyes or their mouth (not all questions are asked with the mouth) "Why should I?" or "What's in it for me?," they are attempting to become self–motivated.*

They are saying, "Mr. Manager, my beam's not tilted yet." "I haven't decided to go." "My switch is not connected yet." "Help me out." "Let me understand more." "Tell me again." "Hit me with it." "Motivate me!"

There's something about the way people are put together that makes it almost impossible for them to do something until they understand why. Think about that for a minute. Have you ever been in a situation where somebody asked you to do something new or unexpected without telling you why. Remember how hard it was to do it, if you did it at all?

I was working in the purchasing department of a company once when the president came in and said, "Would you look at the XYZ account?"

"Sure," I said. "What am I looking for?"

"Just look at it," he said.

"Why?" I asked.

"Never mind. I just want you to go through every invoice that we've had from them for the last year."

"What am I looking for?" I repeated.

"I can't tell you. Just look at it."

I admit this is an extreme case, but it really happened. If he had said he suspected somebody was stealing from us, or a pur-chasing agent was on the take, I could have waded into the project with a purpose. But I didn't know what he wanted. It took me three hours to get sufficiently motivated to go through the file. I did the job because he told me to do it, not because I understood what was to be accomplished. There was little self–motivation to achieve anything. Then when I was finished he had the nerve to ask me to give him an analysis of what I had found.

There was a new husband who didn't know why his bride cut both ends off the ham as she prepared their first Easter dinner. He asked her why and she didn't know, only that she had learned it from her mother. Later, when the mother arrived for dinner, the young husband asked her why she and her daughter cut the ends off of hams. The mother answered that she didn't know why, only that she had learned it from her mother, who would soon arrive to share the dinner with them.

When the grandmother didn't know why either, the young husband was so beside himself with curiosity that he got in his car and drove down to the rest home to ask the great–grandmother why she cut both ends off of hams.

The old lady was almost too feeble to speak, but when she finally understood the question, she explained that when she was a little girl, ovens were so small and hams so big that it was usually necessary to cut the ends off in order to get the hams into the oven. Consider all the wasted ham because nobody bothered to ask why.

### 3) MMFI--Make me feel important!

A colleague of mine was doing some industrial research for a manufacturing company at one time where he was trying to measure morale and attitudes. He interviewed people involved in various stages of the manufacturing process. In one area people were gluing what appeared to be pieces of white plastic onto pieces of hardwood, a very tedious and boring task.

My friend went up to the first worker and asked, "How do you like your job?"

The man said it was a crummy job.

"What are you doing?" my friend asked.

"I'm putting these white things on these hard blocks."

"How do you like the company?"

"I don't," the man said.

"How do you like the benefits?"

"Who cares? They're not so great."

The researcher got similar responses from the next four or five workers. Then he came to a little old lady with her white hair tied up in a bun. She was whistling. The production charts showed that her production rate was 50% above the average.

"How do you like the company?" he asked.

"Great place to work," she responded. "Best job I ever had."

"How do you like the benefits?"

"Super."

"How do you like your boss?"

"Great guy."

"By the way," asked the interviewer. "What do you do?"

"I make pianos."

What she figured out was that she was assembling piano

keys. She knew the fingers of a master or the hands of an inquiring child were going to use her keys to bring joy to themselves and others. She felt important about what she was doing, and was motivated by that feeling of importance.

### 4) Different strokes for different folks

Adolf Hitler was one of the greatest motivators of all time. He got more people to do more things under his control than practically any leader in the history of the world. He made people feel important, and he told them why they should follow him. He knew how to give his people what they thought they wanted. Everyone talks about what Hitler did to his victims, but the incredible thing to note about that notorious villain is how well he motivated the German people. He had the uncanny ability to match the motives of his followers to the things he wanted accomplished. Great motivators can get a group of people to accomplish a single objective for a variety of individual reasons.

Mao Tse-Tung did the same thing in China. He went in with a small band of Chinese communists and took control away from Chiang Kai-shek, who wanted democracy. By our standards Chiang Kai-shek was right and had the best interest of the people at heart, but while he preached democracy and freedom, Mao Tse-Tung was promising food, clothing and shelter—what the people wanted and needed most at the time. Mao won.

Think about the individual in your office most in need of motivation. Do you know the spouse's name? Do you know the age and primary activities of the kids? What hobbies does this person have? How involved is he or she in these hobbies? Do you know where this person would like to be in your company in three years? Does your assessment agree with that? Do you know what this person's net worth is and what he would like it to be? Where does this person like to invest money? What are his or her three greatest fears? If you went out of business, what would this person do to make a living?

# RELATIONSHIP OR EMPLOYEE
# AWARENESS QUESTIONNAIRE

How well do you know your people? Think of a subordinate or someone with whom you have less than an ideal motivational relationship. How would you answer these questions?

1.  Wife's (or husband's) name.


2.  Age and first name of children.


3.  What does he/she like to do off the job?
    List 3 favorite non-work activities.



    Do you know his/her level of performance in each of these areas?



4.  One thing each of his/her children are good at.


5.  What does he/she think next position in company will be?

    How soon will he/she be ready to accept it (in his/her mind)?

    How closely does this agree with your assessment?

6.  Do you know what he/she would do if the company went out of business?


By now you're probably beginning to feel a little inadequate, and I'm not even halfway through my list of questions. The point I am making is that *nobody can motivate a stranger with consistency.* Your ability to motivate people is directly related to how well you know them and how well you're able to interface company goals with their needs and desires. You need to know as much as possible about the people you want to motivate.

And the reverse is true, too. They need to know as much as possible about you, the manager, and the company, too. *Nobody can do what you do unless they know what you know.* You cannot expect people to think the way you think unless they have the information you have.

A typical example is the boss who receives what he considers a bad P&L statement, gets mad, and stuffs it in the drawer so nobody will see it, then walks around with a scowl on his face for an entire month, hoping it will be better next time. He walks up to somebody taking an extra three minutes on a coffee break, reaches out and grabs the person and says, "Don't you understand how much trouble we're in around here?" And the guy says, "No." And the boss decides the employee is irresponsible and doesn't care.

If you want to get more self–motivation in people, get to know them better. If someone in your office is worried about getting bread on the table the next week, you should know about it. If you've got someone with a $10,000 balloon payment due on a piece of real estate next month, you should know about that too. Know what your people need and let them see that you and your organization is a way for them to get it. They may not stay with you forever, but they'll perform better while they do.

# Doing it!

*Everyday everyone needs to know if they have won or lost.*
--Chuck Coonradt

Following are some real examples of companies taking the motivating principles of athletics and applying them in the business world. In fact, the company in this first example through lack of adequate scorekeeping almost lost the whole ballgame.

### Cash flow at a retail lumber yard

On one occasion Western Leadership Group was called in by a retail lumber company with three locations. The company was about to sell its best piece of real estate in an effort to improve cash flow. It had owned that piece of property for over 30 years and the transfer fees and taxes would take a huge chunk of the money. They called us in for a "second opinion" before taking the plunge.

Since we believe there is no such thing as a cash flow problem, our initial investigation uncovered what appeared to be a slackening of credit control, and more serious, a loosening up in purchasing controls affecting inventory turnover.

We recommended a 24–month historical review of receivables and inventory. For the receivables measurement we selected *Working Days of Credit Sales Outstanding and Unpaid.* This was arrived at as follows:

$$\frac{\text{Last 90 Days Credit Sales}}{\text{66 Working Days}} = \begin{array}{l}\text{Average Daily Credit} \\ \text{Sales Outstanding}\end{array}$$

$$\frac{\text{Current Period Ending AR Balance}}{\text{Average Daily Credit Sales Outstanding}} = \begin{array}{c} \text{Working Days of} \\ \text{Credit Sales} \\ \text{Uncollected} \end{array}$$

For the inventory we measured the *Weeks of Inventory on Hand*.

$$\frac{\begin{array}{c}\text{Last 13 Weeks Sales X}\\ \text{Cost of Goods Sold \%}\end{array}}{13} = \begin{array}{c}\text{Average Weekly Cost}\\ \text{of Goods Sold in \$}\end{array}$$

$$\frac{\text{Period Ending Inventory}}{\text{Average Weekly COG in \$}} = \begin{array}{c}\text{Weeks of Inventory}\\ \text{on Hand}\end{array}$$

These measurements were not very unusual, but are excellent Results to Resource Ratios.

We found that the *Working Days of Credit Sales Outstanding and Unpaid* had grown from a low of 43 days to a high at the present time of 67 days. That increase in 24 days of sales outstanding tied up just under a quarter of a million dollars of operating capital.

Our findings in the inventory area were even more remarkable. In a previous year's peak selling time of optimum turnover, the inventory had been reduced to the equivalent of 8.3 *Weeks of Inventory on Hand.* No one could recall that there had been any unusual problems in filling orders, no increase in out–of–stock items, no increase in unhappy customers. The inventory, however, had been allowed to grow to 16.7 weeks in stock. The additional seven weeks of inventory tied up an additional $200,000 of operating capital. In just two areas, the introduction of scorekeeping––of keeping historical measurements––uncovered the opportunity to recover almost half a million dollars!

We recommended to management that they hold up on the sale of the real estate and get to work on the receivables and inventory. Thirteen weeks later receivables had been reduced to 53 (from 67) days outstanding, releasing $150,000 in working capital. Eighteen weeks later the inventory level was back to 12 weeks, releasing an additional $100,000 of operating capital. It was no longer necessary to sell the piece of real estate.

Let me emphasize that we are not talking about magic techniques to swamp the lucky businessman with fistfuls of cash, though I have witnessed some seemingly miraculous results when proper scorekeeping methods were implemented. What we are talking about is players or competitors gaining an increased awareness of each opportunity to score.

Charting measurements over time, sometimes called a historical review, can magnify the understanding of measurement information many times.

But don't make the mistake of oversimplifying the problem. A golf course may be 7200 yards long with a par of 72 strokes. You may score par by averaging 100 yards per stroke. The hundred yard drives are a cinch, but what about the hundred yard putts? Only by accurate scorekeeping and measurement of every part of the game do you improve each part of the game and come out a winner. Your drives will go well over 100 yards, and your putts will never get close to the 100–yard mark, but as you keep score on each part of the game your averages will improve. The same principle applies in business.

## Increased profitability for a communications firm

Sometimes it's important to spend more time getting the rules straight before we start to play. I was involved in such an opportunity in 1975. A public communications company called me in to help with budget plans for 1976. The firm had been languishing for years in a rather flat but still acceptable profit picture. Their operating profit had been bouncing between $1.4 and $1.9 million a year for four years. In the most recent year, it had dropped to $1.7 million.

It was September, and the chief executive called me in to see if I could help get their fall budget and planning session off to a better start.

In our preliminary discussions the chief executive discussed what the experts were saying about the stock market, and what he thought were the plans of the competition for the coming year, the relationship with the holding company, and a dozen other irrelevant items, used in previous years to get the budgeting process underway. It became clear to me that we needed to clarify the rules before the game began.

I asked the chief executive what kind of profit picture he would like for the new year. He responded by saying the best they had ever done was $2.25 million.

"Would you like that again next year?" I asked.

"I don't know," he said. "I haven't finished studying all the economic predictions." He also indicated a string of unprofitable Januarys due to the fact that the budgeting for the new year which was started in September was never finished by January.

"Would you like to earn that much?" I persisted, realizing that his own internal will was among the most important factors in that company's profit planning.

"Yes," he finally said. "I believe I'd like to take a shot at it." And so we outlined a $2.25 million operating plan.

"What percentage of your profit comes from your major operating division?" I asked, and he said 86% had been the traditional contribution of the major division. We assigned 86% of the profit to the flagship division.

"Is it fair?" he asked.

"Do you believe it is?" I responded.

"I do," he said.

The next division accounted for just under 10%, so we rounded its share up to 10%, and the third division accounted for 4%. We allocated 100% of the corporate profit goal based on the historical percentage of revenue contribution. The president then mentioned all the other areas of responsibility that consumed various amounts of his budget. We agreed after a brief discussion that those areas would be subordinated to the three profit–making divisions, and would not be discussed further until the plans for the profit–producing divisions had been established.

Safely convinced in my own mind that he and I were in accord, I left him that Friday afternoon looking forward to a Monday morning group meeting with the division heads.

At the Monday meeting he said, "Gentlemen, I've prepared the budget and I'm going to ask you to meet some very simple requirements."

He then presented each of the division heads with an envelope containing the total net dollars of operating profit expected from each man. After the initial yelling and screaming subsided, the men went back to their offices and in half the normal time prepared operating plans that would get the chief executive officer the amount of profit he asked for. The operating plans were finished by Thanksgiving, whereas in previous years they had not been finished before the end of the year. Though that initial meeting was tense, it was as it should have been, the chief executive communicating clearly with his top lieutenants, telling them exactly what he expected them to do.

The company did not achieve the $2.25 million goal that year. It achieved $3.4 million, due mostly to two things. One, the early completion of the operating plans enabled the divisions to be off and running by the first of the year, whereas in previous years the plans hadn't been agreed upon until the end of January. Two, the general manager of the flagship division began to strum the strings of his imagination and created one of the greatest incentive purchase programs in that company's history. He said he knew what he had to do, and because of that went way past the budget. That year the meetings focused on profit and growth rather than the usual nitpicking through expenses and having a generally repressive, negative time. With the profit goals clearly established at the outset, many of the negative, unnecessary activities were pushed aside. The lieutenants loved the new system. They had clearly defined goals and a way to win.

The leadership had come from the top. It was specific, direct and intense.

The chief executive later confessed to me that he didn't sleep well the Sunday night before that meeting, and that the entire weekend had been one of the most miserable of his entire life. As we laughed about it 15 months later over a record profit and loss statement, he told me his profit goal for the coming year was $4.4 million. And he had previously rejected my suggestion of a minimum 15% annual increase in profit dollars as being too tough and unrealistic.

**Improving maintenance for a trucking firm**

One time we were called into a $10 million a year trucking company to work on maintenance problems. First, we measured maintenance costs (labor and parts) as a percentage of total billings. Although this measurement was nearly twice the national average for similar firms, the measurements didn't show any dramatic fluctuations, so they were not very useful. We didn't have anything to compare the measurements against.

So we devised a non–standard measurement––the average miles between breakdowns. We borrowed this idea from the U.S. Defense Department, which for years has been measuring the time between failures of its defense systems. We did the same thing with the trucks.

It was a self–administered scorekeeping system with the mechanics taking readings from the odometers of each truck when there was a breakdown. Routine maintenance and servicing were not included.

The mechanic or the supervisor of maintenance in each of the garage facilities built his own scorecard for each vehicle in his care. It was very simple, not cumbersome at all. The man in charge would simply subtract the odometer reading from the reading at the previous breakdown to get the miles between breakdowns.

Once the system was operational, we discovered one service terminal which needed immediate attention with its trucks averaging only 750 miles between breakdowns. For the first time the company had an accurate record of how the various repair facilities were doing in comparison to each other. The system also enabled us to compare the service records of trucks from different manufacturers. We could also compare parts performance—spark plugs, axles, tires, etc.

As a result of the new miles–between–breakdown measurement, the company increased the rotation frequency of vehicles and reduced overall transportation repair costs by 1.2% of sales. In that $10 million company, that resulted in an annual savings of $125,000.

Again, no magic in the cure. We just helped good, solid employees increase their awareness of opportunities to take better shots.

I believe people who have sufficient comparative awareness of their performance relative to their goals will do the proper thing.

## Improving the customer's opportunity to give you money

We were called in to consult a company that built custom overhead cranes for materials handling. As we began the investigation we took a look at receivables, as we always do. Although receivables are normally updated monthly, they must be watched daily.

The standard way to track receivables is an aging report—dividing the money owed you into 30, 60 and 90 day blocks. The aging report shows what percentage of the money owed you falls into each of the categories. When you confront the average collections manager on the status of his receivables he will give you some evasive rhetoric regarding percentages—that it is up 2%, or down 2%, it has shifted here, or there, and the total amount over 90 days is X. Good information, but you don't know where you are headed, if the situation is really getting better, or worse.

The first measurement we added for the crane company was the number of days of business outstanding—the amount of business we've done in the last 90 days that we have not been paid for. This measurement is concise, flexible, easily measured and gives rapid feedback. It tells you how good you are at getting the money owed you, and if you are getting better or worse at collecting it.

As we began to track the number of days of business outstanding we quickly recognized the company had a real problem with receivables. The number of days of business outstanding was approaching 90.

As we began to discuss how the problem might be corrected, a casual slip of the tongue caught our immediate attention. Someone said, "I bet if we could get our invoices out faster, we'd get paid better."

"Tell me more," said the Western Leadership consultant. "How long does it take now?"

What he heard was altogether too typical, an observation management response—a lot of talk about one invoice here, another there, two that had this or that problem. People involved in management by observation always cite the examples that reinforce their personal point of view. It was evident that nobody really knew how soon the invoices were sent out. No measurement existed.

Our man set up a simple scorecard to be completed by the invoice clerk under the direction of the controller. They began to identify and track the number of days required from job completion date until the invoice was in the mail to the customer.

On the first batch of 20 invoices, the average processing time was 13 working days. The process of checking against the bid, auditing, price checking and double checking was causing a full month's delay in the customer's opportunity to pay.

We all know the customer is never eager to pay, regardless of when the bill comes. But we decided the money would come faster if the invoices were sent out sooner, closer to the work completion dates. We also reasoned that most of the customers paid in some kind of billing cycle and that if we could get invoices to them sooner, we'd increase our chances of catching an earlier cycle.

The scorecard told us the invoicing performance was not up to our expectations. Armed with that information the controller began to explore the causes of the slow invoicing and how the situation might be corrected. Using additional scorecarding, the controller began to study the invoicing process, uncovering the bottlenecks. One by one he identified the problem areas and began to snip away at them. Within six weeks the average number of working days to produce an invoice to the customer had gone from 13 down to 3. We had eliminated almost two weeks out of the time required to get our invoice to the customer. Within six weeks we saw a noticeable improvement in collections.

## Controlling seasonal unprofitability in a bottling company

Another great example of using scorekeeping to bring seasonal fluctuations under control occurred in a local bottling company. They retained our services during a marginal profit year in an effort to curtail losses after the first of the year. The company traditionally had strong sales and profitability during the summer and fall months, peaking at the holiday season. After the first of the year, however, the company always entered a period of 30 to 90 days in the red.

In selecting a Results to Resource Ratio measurement, we identified two items that did not fluctuate with inflation: costs or economy. The sales manager began to track each route or truck on the basis of cases delivered per gallons of fuel consumed by the truck. Adjustments were made for propane and diesel powered vehicles, also for flatbed and gooseneck trailers. Almost immediately there was an increase in the number of cases delivered per gallon of gas consumed, and for the first time in its history, the company operated in the black during January and February. When management saw this working, they introduced a cases/mile scorecard for their routes which enabled them to decrease labor costs in accordance with seasonal drops in sales. This one measurement alone enabled the company to reduce delivery costs by 15% with no appreciable decrease in sales revenues.

## Shifting the emphasis from people to dollars for the March of Dimes

One of our clients was the volunteer chairman of a March of Dimes telethon. The most money the group had ever raised was $78,000. In the past the goals of the person in charge had been measured in number of people contacted and other activities related to the fund–raising process.

We implemented a new program in which the emphasis was shifted from people contacted to dollars raised. We set up a tracking system based on performance in past years. The measurement system had the ability to update the progress hourly during the telethon.

With the new system in place a goal of $100,000 was set,

$22,000 higher than any amount previously raised. That first year they raised $110,000. Within three years the telethon was raising more than $200,000 a year, compared to a high of $78,000 before a sound measurement system was adopted.

## Even the waste can be measured

A fencing company asked us to help improve its overall productivity. The first thing we did was set up a non–inflationary measurement for the entire company. We charted pounds of product per person–hour. We included management and clerical employees as well as production workers in the measurement. We started out at 127 pounds per person–hour, and after four months playing *The Game of Work*, productivity had increased to 196 pounds per person–hour.

As we implemented the tracking system, it was necessary to devise several intermediate scorecards. One of the greatest challenges was the scrap problem associated with the drawing process where six– and eight–gauge galvanized wire is drawn into nine– and eleven–gauge wire to be made into basket weave fencing. The supervisor in charge of this drawing operation had no idea whether he was winning or losing on a daily basis, and he had no way to measure it, or so he thought.

He was in a situation where it is hard to win. The goal seemed to be to minimize losses in a situation where dies would wear out and the gauge was inconsistent most of the time. Very little was ever right about the operation. It seemed there was no way to win. From a financial standpoint, the president of the organization was well aware that the company was spending thousands of dollars a month in hauling costs alone to dispose of the scrap wire.

When the operation was at peak performance two nine–cubic–yard dumpsters were filled daily with scrap resulting from broken dies, broken runs, operator error, and a variety of other causes.

At the suggestion of one of my associates, the company installed a weighing device to track the scrap and provide immediate feedback to the operator. It was soon discovered that some of the operators were more wasteful than others, that some were not suited for that particular job. Adjustments were made. Within six weeks of installation of the weighing device, the amount of scrap had been reduced from two bins a day to two bins a week, an almost 80% reduction with the logical conclusion that there was an increased amount of wire going into finished galvanized fencing. And the scrap disposal costs were cut by

$40,000 a year.

## A simple measurement to reduce shelf-stocking costs

Cases per person-hour has been a good item to track in distributor warehouses and retail stores, particularly grocery stores. We convinced the assistant manager of a small closely-held grocery chain to track every delivery over a period of weeks. We found that productivity ranged from a low of 34 cases per person-hour to a high of over 60 cases per person-hour. We recognized immediately that the workers' goals had never been expressed in productivity, but rather in survival until the end of the shift. We could see that in filling the schedule, 1,500-case loads were being done in 30 person-hours at a rate of over 50 cases per person-hour. Several days later a 1,000-case load delivered to the same store would require the same number of person-hours—evidence that Dr. Parkinson's laws are indeed at work.

As the crews became aware they were being tracked, production picked up. The crews were allowed to go home when the work was finished. And management amply determined that they could pay the crew on a piece rate basis which allowed more flexibility in scheduling. Once that was firmly in place, shelf-stocking costs dropped by 27%.

## An ideal tracking system for new salespeople

Once I was contacted by a new independent sales agent who was not meeting his sales goals, not even coming close to his expectations. In discussing the problem our attention focused on two ideas. One, that if we asked a new salesman to sell one contract his first month, and two his second month, we were telling him that if he wanted to get stroked he had to double his productivity in one month—his first month, the hardest month of his career. That was no good.

The other idea we kept talking about, that used in the maintenance example with the trucking firm, was something I recalled from a purchasing class in college, about a government specification on weapon systems called "mean time between failures." We synthesized the two ideas into what we called MDBS (mean days between sales). We created the following preliminary goals program for new sales people:

1) Go get your first sale as quickly as you can, wherever you can, from whomever you can, for whatever price you can. (We

even considered taking a lower price in an effort to give the new salesperson a good closing experience as soon as possible.)

2) Get your second sale in less time than you got the first one.

3) Get your third sale in less than the average of the first two.

4) Continue to beat your average.

After a dismal first 90 days when he was on the verge of resignation, this young man implemented the MDBS tracking system. At the end of a year he was recognized by his company as the national rookie of the year.

This MDBS formula has worked better than any other start–up goal–setting process we know of and it is getting more people into solid sales production in more areas of the country than anything I know of.

The MDBS enables the sales manager to coach the hitter individually. It gives the new people a chance to feel the excitement of success through gradual improvement in their production.

## In Conclusion

The principles discussed here have resulted in improvement and increased profitability in every imaginable type of business or organized activity. These principles are timeless. They work as well in business as they do in athletics and recreation.

One word of caution. These kinds of successes are the result of a careful presentation of the measurement concept, after conditioning the players to want to be measured. Players must be sold on these measurement concepts before they will work.

Once a person is sold on the value of scorekeeping, and that person's personal goals are consistent with the overall goals of the company where he or she works, the Field of Play is clearly defined and Results to Resource Ratios are in place, allowing that person to know if he or she is winning or losing every day, the increased productivity of that individual will be phenomenal.

When the principles in this book are applied in the work place, people no longer only pay for the privilege of working harder than they will work for pay. Your *Game of Work* becomes a favorite activity, attracting the focus, enthusiasm and energy that was once reserved for recreational pursuits only.